10 Dilemmas
in Teaching with
Discussion

D1166155

10 Dilemmas in Teaching with Discussion

Managing Integral Instruction

Jody S. Piro
Western Connecticut State University

INFORMATION AGE PUBLISHING, INC.
Charlotte, NC • www.infoagepub.com

Library of Congress Cataloging-in-Publication Data

A CIP record for this book is available from the Library of Congress
http://www.loc.gov

ISBN: 978-1-68123-515-8 (Paperback)
         978-1-68123-516-5 (Hardcover)
         978-1-68123-517-2 (ebook)

Copyright © 2016 Information Age Publishing Inc.

All rights reserved. No part of this publication may be reproduced, stored in a
retrieval system, or transmitted, in any form or by any means, electronic, mechanical,
photocopying, microfilming, recording or otherwise, without written permission
from the publisher.

Printed in the United States of America

Contents

Introduction

The test of a first-rate intelligence is the ability to hold two opposing ideas in mind at the same time and still retain the ability to function.

—F. Scott Fitzgerald (1945)

Constructivist instructors regularly face pedagogical dilemmas, such as complying with external standards while also constructing their own conceptions of pedagogy; or giving students an active voice in instruction and assessment and also ensuring learning has concrete outcomes (Nikitina, 2012; Tillema & Kremer-Hayon, 2005; Windschitl, 2002). The complex nature of constructivist classrooms leads to instructional dilemmas with which teachers must regularly cope and manage. As part of constructivist pedagogy, there are dilemmas of practices and goals when leading discussions in classrooms. Yet, these dilemmas allow instructors to actively reflect upon the connections between their professional thinking and strategies (Tillema & Kremer-Hayon, 2005) for managing discussion dilemmas. Reflecting upon dilemmas in discussion establishes a potent process for understanding one's perspectives and beliefs about instruction (Windschitl, 2002) and for deliberately restructuring instruction to embrace those dilemmas for integral practice.

10 Dilemmas in Teaching with Discussion, pages vii–xviii
Copyright © 2016 by Information Age Publishing
All rights of reproduction in any form reserved.

Instructors use discussion in their teaching for many reasons. One common rationale for using discussion relates to promoting democratic learning environments in classrooms. Using discussion in instruction may facilitate spaces where students can engage with difficult and opposing ideas as a form of shared inquiry. Discussion is part of a larger curricular goal that intersects the two aspirations of diversity of perspectives and democratic inquiry in that it challenges stereotypes and assumptions through student interactions (Piro & Anderson, 2015). An essential goal of discussion is increased personal understanding of difficult issues through social learning. Discussion pedagogy engages students with issues that surpass the self and connects them with larger societal problems, allowing them to expand their perspectives and increase their worldviews of difficult issues. Teaching with discussion may advance the capability to connect the classroom to the public-sphere through the use of critical and reasoned discourse (Dahlberg, 2001; Dryek, 1996) and through purposely dealing with controversial issues in the classroom (Hess, 2009). Instruction with discussion may also promote democratic learning spaces in classrooms (Brookfield & Preskill, 2012; Hess, 2009). Linda Darling-Hammond (1996) stated:

> America's capacity to survive as a democracy...rests on the kind of education that arms people with an intelligence capable of free and independent thought...that helps people to build common ground across diverse experiences and ideas...that enables all people to find and act on who they are, what their passions, gifts, and talents may be, what they care about, and how they want to make a contribution to each other and the world. (p.5){/ext}

Viewed in this light, discussion pedagogy may help students to navigate taken-for-granted ideas and habits of thought, increasing the potential for connecting dialogue and democracy.

Nevertheless, teaching with discussion is a complex and sometimes ambiguous endeavor (Anderson & Piro, 2016). Using discussion pedagogy promotes perturbation, disturbance, and disequilibrium (Doll, 1993) as natural and anticipated outcomes of instruction. Instructors using discussion often feel pulled between desirable, but seemingly contradictory, outcomes for their students: for example, wanting students to participate but also wanting them to learn to listen to others' viewpoints; hoping that they will dialogue but also wanting them to pose questions with each other; expecting they will use the text to ground their opinions and also valuing students' personal experiences as they relate to the topic under discussion. Similarly, instructors using discussion must manage instructional dilemmas: focusing on the process of discussion but also having an eye on the possible products of the discussion, such as outside actions or a culminating project;

wanting to provide structure to help students understand expectations and increase student engagement; and also valuing organic, less structured dialogues that highlight student interest in the topic.

These contradictions may be met with a problem-solving stance leading to an either/or consequence, choosing one pedagogical goal over another. Yet, the paradoxical outcomes and instructional choices in discussion, though opposing, are mutually desirable. In fact, each side of the dilemma relies on the other. These types of problems for discussion outcomes and goals are not really problems. They are instructional dilemmas, and dilemmas simply need management.

Managing Integral Instruction: Dilemmas in Discussion Instruction

> *The puzzle in a paradox serves as an impulse; it energises our minds to "jump the rails" in search of a reconciling insight.*
>
> —Pascale, (1990, p. 110)

The integrative thinking necessary to manage discussion teaching finds roots in various disciplines. For example, research in neurology has suggested that information provided to humans' nervous systems must be relayed in one of two directions—one system producing more emotional and instinctual responses to the information and one more rational (LeDoux, 1998)—leading to a binary analysis of information by the brain that requires conscious integration. Koestler (1967) discussed the importance of reconciling atomistic and holistic (or part/whole) approaches in biological systems, while Capra (2003) theorized complexity in whole systems thinking. In Eastern traditions, Taoism (Lao Tsu, 1972) embraced the duality of life and the balance of opposites, as did Jung (1986) in Western psychological traditions who suggested that humans were constantly hurled between opposing forces that required an integral approach to both oppositions. Organizational theory (Lawrence & Lorsch, 1967; Johnson, 1998; McGregor, 1957; Martin, 2009; Pascale, 1990) demonstrated the limitations of using oppositional thinking and the value of more integrative approaches in the culture of organizations.

For the conceptual model to analyze the dilemmas of discussion pedagogy, I use a polarity management framework. A polarity management model, first set forth by Johnson (1992; 1998), suggests that polarities are ongoing issues—ones that are unavoidable and unsolvable. Polarities, or as I refer to them, dilemmas, are often addressed with "problem-solving" skills. Rather, dilemmas need to be managed, not solved like a problem. Problems usually have a right answer; whereas dilemmas have multiple answers. There are two fundamental questions to ask when encountering difficult dilemmas. Is this a problem we can "solve" or is it an ongoing polarity we must manage well? And, are there two poles which are interdependent (Johnson, 1998, p. 2)? If the answers to both questions are yes, polarity management offers a process to manage the dilemma.

To use polarity management, one must move beyond *either/or* to *both/and thinking*. A polarity has two or more right answers diametrically opposed, yet interdependent upon each other. For example, some common examples of dilemmas faced by all leaders and organizations are (Freeman, 2004):

- Stability/change
- Uniqueness/uniformity
- Quality/cost
- Part/whole
- Candor/diplomacy
- Centralized/decentralized
- Privacy/openness
- Individual/team
- Employee needs/organization needs
- Compassion/accountability
- Relationships/productivity
- Planned/emergent

Johnson (1998) suggests that polarities also occur in everyday circumstances. For example, when teaching a child how to interact with a friend, there are two polar and interdependent values: teaching the child to be concerned about someone else and also teaching to be concerned about herself. Taking care of only one of those poles does not lead to a satisfactory relationship; both are necessary. In a friend relationship, one needs to attend to the friend's needs and one's own as well (Johnson, 1998, p. 4). A second everyday circumstance regards parenting. Johnson asks:

> You are a parent during a holiday season in which each of your 3 children is to receive a gift. Should you give each one something that is unique to them and responds to their interests and desires at the moment? Or, should you pay attention to giving gifts of approximately equal value so they will all feel that they were treated equally? (Johnson, 1998, p. 4)

This dilemma demonstrates a polarity for parents to respond to both the uniqueness of children and the value of treating them equally.

Johnson further demonstrated another polarity management mode—the example of breathing. The polarities of inhaling and exhaling appear to be opposite functions. Yet it would be unproductive not to recognize the reciprocal relationship between the body's attempt to collect oxygen and its opposite attempt to rid itself of carbon dioxide. Inhalation and exhalation are paradoxically connected into a whole function—breathing—that cannot persist without both poles.

Functional discussions produce their own sets of dilemmas that must be managed. Laiken (2002) extended the use of polarity management more specifically to discussions and dialogues. She studied the polarity of action and reflection as dilemmas within work-style differences within discussion. Convergent approaches to work are often reinforced by pressures to quickly make decisions and move forward. On the other hand, divergent thinking can help expand the possibilities, but may be considered less strategic and deliberate by those who are task-oriented. By managing these dilemmas during discussions with adult learners, Laiken found that balance was achieved between task and process activities and that difference could be viewed in a productive way.

As a result of my own practice and collaborations with others (Anderson & Piro, 2016; Anderson & Piro, in press), I developed a set of dilemmas to use in discussion pedagogy. Table I.1 illustrates ten key dilemmas of discussion pedagogy, each with its own value and each which is interdependent upon the other. Neither side of the dilemma can produce operational

TABLE I.1 10 Key Dilemmas in Teaching with Discussion	
Participating	Witnessing
Democracy	Safety
Structured	Unstructured
Scholarlines	Personal Experienc
Cognitive Learning	Social/Emotional Learning
Product	Process
Relational Learning	Personal Learning
Autonomy	Open-Mindedness
Dialoguing	Questioning
Whole Group	Small Group

discussion on its own. Both sides of the dilemmas are desirable for effective discussion and are further discussed in the sections that follow.

Participating and Witnessing

In discussions, there is a polarity between students participating in verbal dialogue and witnessing the dialogue. This polarity encompasses oppositional student goals to participate by speaking and providing measured viewpoints and to active listening and reflecting in a witnessing modality. Participating in the speaking component of discussion provides a forum for students to advance ideas, and witnessing may lead to expanded perspectives.

Safety and Democracy

Discussion of difficult topics may increase the likelihood of conflict within the classroom. Some teachers value the outcomes of discussion where students regularly engage with ideas that interrupt or contrast their own assumptions as a part of their mission to promote democratic learning spaces that mirror civil life in a democracy. Other teachers hope to encourage safe spaces for learning where students experience comfort and trust. These two values may become dilemmas for instruction with discussion.

Structured and Unstructured

Structuring discussions in varying forms to allow input from multiple parties, provide pedagogical variance, and encourage participation from normally silent students are positive interventions. Yet the value of organic discussions which do not follow strictly structured guidelines and spontaneously move with student interest is a valued process of discussion pedagogy.

Scholarliness and Personal Experience

Grounding student dialogue in course content and readings by asking students to refer to course content when they dialogue is a goal for informed discussions such as a Socratic Seminar, yet the value of personal experience within difficult discussions is equally valid.

Cognitive and Social/Emotional Learning

Thinking processes, such as critical analysis, problem-solving, meta-cognition, remembering, and comprehending are all common cognitive outcomes of discussion. Yet, the value of social and emotional learning, such as compassion and empathy, conflict resolution, and self and other awareness, are valuable outcomes of discussion instruction.

Product and Process

The process of the discussion is important; attending to the above dilemmas within the practice of discussion, allowing for risk, encouraging self-growth and metacognition—each of these process-oriented instructional choices make for a functioning discussion. Yet, many instructors also want a culmination to the discussion, perhaps even action based upon the discussion. It is not enough to simply raise consciousness; action culminating from the discussion is valued.

Relational and Personal Learning

Pursuing both relational knowledge, the ability to understand and dialogue in contexts with people representing diverse ideas that may differ from one's own perspectives, and personal knowledge, reflection and knowledge of one's own thinking, values and assumptions and individual creativity, are both valid outcomes for students in discussion pedagogy and are, in fact, interdependent outcomes.

Autonomy and Open-Mindedness

Instructors hope that students will develop the ability to have rational confidence in their beliefs, values, and inferences, or what might be termed intellectual autonomy (Paul, 1993) while simultaneously encouraging open-mindedness, or the ability to consider new and differing perspectives (Dewey, 1933, 1944).

Dialoguing and Questioning

There is a dilemma between the pedagogical goals of wanting students to dialogue and to pose questions. Dialogues of student opinions, by themselves, are incomplete. Using varying forms of questioning is needed as well. By questioning, students learn to recognize their own and others' limitations in content and analysis.

_____

Whole Group and Small Groups

The last dilemma is between whole class discussion and small group discussions. Both forms are desirable and both are inter-related. Whole group discussions allow common coverage of content and common group processes. Small group discussions promote more engagement and more local knowledge.

_____

Next Steps

Highlighting the differences between the dilemmas of discussion pedagogy is only a first step. Next, polarities need to be mapped to determine the positive benefits and negative consequences of each dilemma. According to Johnson (1992), polarity management has some essential steps which may be applied to discussion pedagogy. First, identify which components of the discussion are problems to solve and which are instructional dilemmas. An example of a problem to solve in discussion pedagogy is the choice of topic or the guiding question that initiates the discussion. Instructors must decide which content best suits discussion pedagogy and which questions will intrigue and create interest. A second problem is whether discussion is the best form of pedagogy for the content. An additional problem to solve is how much time will be spent within the discussion. These are each problems that instructors must solve prior to engaging students in the discussion.

Dilemmas within discussion pedagogy are those values from the previous section which are not problems, though they are mutually related contradictions that need to be managed rather than solved. Naming those dilemmas is a key element of polarity management. The next phase to manage the dilemma is to create a polarity map (Johnson, 1992)—or what I call a dilemma map. A dilemma map provides a visual of the strengths and weaknesses that come from focusing only on each side of the pole. Johnson (1998) stated:

> Polarities to manage are sets of positions which can't function well independently. Because the two sides of a polarity are interdependent, you cannot choose one as a "solution" and neglect the other. The objective of polarity management perspective is to get the best of both opposites while avoiding the limits of each. (p. xviii)

Johnson's (1998) point is that each side of a dilemma has both strengths and weaknesses. Dilemma maps have four quadrants. The upper two quadrants demonstrate the positive outcomes of using the polarity. The bottom quadrants demonstrate the negative results from over-relying on that side

Positive Quadrants

+ Upper Left	+ Upper Right
Positive attributes of this side of the dilemma	Positive attributes of the other side of the dilemma
One side of dilemma in discussion	**Other side of dilemma in discussion**
Negative attributes of this side of the dilemma	Negative attributes of the other side of the dilemma
– Lower Left	– Lower Right

Negative Quadrants

Table I.1   Sample dilemma map.

of the pole. The goal of polarity management is to stay in the two upper quadrants when possible (Johnson, 1998, p. 81) or, when negative expressions of the dilemma are being expressed, to move from the negative quadrants into the positive quadrants. A general sample of a dilemma map appears in Figure I.1.

How to Use This Book

Each chapter focuses on one of ten dilemmas in teaching with discussion. The dilemma is introduced and background information regarding the instructional dilemma is offered. A dilemma map visual—informed by Johnson's (1998) polarity management system—is provided, and the issues of the map are developed. A text box highlights the clues for student behaviors that may alert instructors to intentionally move to the other side of the map when they notice the behaviors occurring. A final dilemma map represents the movement from negative quadrants to positive quadrants within the map. The chapter ends with questions for instructors and their students to investigate regarding each side of the dilemma.

Instructors might use this book in several ways. First, consider the ten dilemmas. Is there one side of the dilemma that you use more frequently while teaching with discussion? If so, target the opposite side of the dilemma map for a semester to intentionally create the inter-related goals or outcomes for your students. For example, if you are expecting and your students are consistently dialoguing and expressing opinions in your discussions, consider targeting the opposite pole—questioning—for the semester. Can you provide scaffolding to assist your students to infuse more self-questioning within their discussions? To increase questioning among students' peers? After both sides of the dilemma are a natural part of your classroom norms for instructing with discussion, move to another dilemma.

Another way to use the book is to select one dilemma map that has been systemically absent from or underused in your discussion instruction. For example, if you have not consciously addressed intellectual autonomy and open-mindedness as central outcomes for discussion pedagogy, focus on that one dilemma. Foster an awareness of and frameworks for producing both sides of the dilemma in discussion instruction for a set timeframe. Notice if your students slip into the negative quadrants of one side of the dilemma map and intentionally change your instructional focus so that the other side is acknowledged and more purposefully expressed within discussion.

Consider sharing the dilemma map you are using with your students along with the questions at the end of the chapter, which will make for interesting discussion themselves. In my own practice, I find that explicitly teaching the dilemmas with the students produces better outcomes. When students know your explicit goals for teaching with discussion, they may help you to identify when one side of the dilemma map is being expressed negatively, thereby helping you to know when to move to the instructional choices on the other side of the map. The final questions in each chapter may be used to clearly teach the dilemmas of discussion to students. As instructors choose to work with a set of dilemmas in their instruction, these questions can provide an overarching foundation to the work; in essence, creating a meta-discussion about discussion. This meta-analysis of the processes gently nudges students into reflection of the dilemma prior to the actual action of the discussion. Furthermore, using the dilemma questions as a focus for the meta-discussion of the discussion demonstrates integral thinking as an underpinning to dilemma mapping.

Last, use the book as an ongoing resource before each semester. All instructors who use discussion as pedagogy must confront these dilemmas in their instruction or risk unconsciously over-emphasizing one side of the instructional dilemma. By regularly referencing the dilemma maps prior to and during instruction, instructors may become more intentional and integral in their choices for discussions.

As a final note, there are several dilemmas that work on both a macro and micro level. For example, democracy works as a dilemma with safety as mutual outcomes of discussion pedagogy. However, creating democratic learning environments is also an element of several other dilemmas, such as the participating side of the participating and witnessing dilemma. Similarly, open-mindedness is an element of several sides of dilemmas, such as witnessing and social-emotional learning. Yet, it further stands as a key side of a dilemma opposed to intellectual autonomy. In essence, some dilemmas are discrete polarities of discussion *and* individual components of other dilemmas. Both/and integral thinking is necessary to use dilemma mapping with discussion instruction.

Note

Parts of this book appeared in an earlier journal article published by Cogent Education. Piro, J. S., & Anderson, G. (2015). Managing the paradoxes of discussion pedagogy. *Cogent Education, 2*(1), 1–10.

1

Participating and Witnessing

This chapter deals with the interconnected goals of participating and witnessing within discussion pedagogy. Instructors want students to participate in discussions. Actively taking part in the discussion allows students to advance ideas and make connections to the readings. The ability to participate civilly with others is a dispositional outcome of discussion. Yet, instructors also want students to listen and to actively witness and reflect upon others' perspectives and thoughts. These goals are interdependent within discussions and must be reciprocally valued. A dilemma map demonstrates the positives and negatives of both sides of the dilemma. In addition, clues when an instructor is over-relying on one side of the map are provided and a final visual demonstrates the movement from the lower quadrant to the appropriate upper quadrant when an instructor notices negative behaviors from the lower quadrants. The chapter ends with questions for discussion regarding participating and witnessing as mutual goals.

10 Dilemmas in Teaching with Discussion, pages 1–7
Copyright © 2016 by Information Age Publishing
All rights of reproduction in any form reserved.

Dilemma Map of Participating and Witnessing in Discussion

Participating and witnessing within discussions are mapped in Figure 1.1. In the upper left quadrant, the positive benefits of participating are listed. In the upper right quadrant, the positive benefits of witnessing in discussions are given. In the lower left quadrant are the negative consequences of participating, and in the lower right quadrant the negative consequences of witnessing in discussions are provided.

In the upper left quadrant of this dilemma map, the participating benefits of discussion are listed. A positive element of participating in discussion

Positive Quadrants

+ Upper Left	+ Upper Right
Civility Integrity Courage Responsibility to group/ democratic learning	Active listening Reflection Empathy/humility Open-mindedness and courage
Participating	**Witnessing**
Action without reflection Ego-centric thinking Indifference Soft bulling/teasing	Reflection without action Meekness Responsibility only to self
− Lower Left	− Lower Right

Negative Quadrants

Figure 1.1 Dilemma map of participating and witnessing.

is the possibility of civil discourse emerging. John Dewey said that democracy begins with conversation (e.g., Farrell, 1959), and participating in that conversation is an essential component. Yet, dialogue requires participants to display integrity, being true to one's own beliefs and values (Paul, 1993), and to understand their own opinions as they relate to the dialogue (Phillips, 2001). Last, participating in discussion is an essential step in creating democratic learning spaces in group dynamics that encourage and expect participants to actively engage in crucial matters.

A focus on the upper right quadrant, the positives of witnessing, suggests that witnessing within a discussion has value too. Active listening is a skill that may be explicitly addressed as a goal for this side of the dilemma map. Active listening includes listening to competing points of view, considering new evidence, and treating each other as political equals (McAvoy & Hess, 2013). Reflection of others' dialogue may allow students to recognize when their own attitudes and values are overly egocentric, not aligned with current research, or restricted in other ways. Reflection precedes action. With reflection comes humility—an understanding of the limitations of one's own perspectives—and empathy—the ability to feel other's positions with compassion (Paul, 1993). Open-mindedness is characterized by welcoming new ways of thinking as one would welcome a guest into one's home (Rodgers, 2002) and the courage to face ideas with which one may have a strong emotional reaction (Paul, 1993) or strong distaste.

The lower left quadrant represents the negative outcomes of focusing solely on students' active participation in discussion. Students who participate without reflection may not engage with contradictions and competing values, preferring their own self-centered ones as an easier route to listening and understanding multiple perspectives. This lack of engagement with contrary ideas may encourage indifference and disinterest in concepts and values that students do not hold, resulting in little exchange between students and a self-referential dynamic that leads to action without the benefit of reflection.

The lower right quadrant represents the negative possibilities of only witnessing within discussion pedagogy. Students who only witness at the expense of participating and demonstrating their perspectives risk non-action or non-informed action, not only because they do not engage in action beyond their personal perspectives, but because others in the class do not hear their reasoned reflections and those students may act with uninformed perspectives. This intellectual meekness does allow the student to remain in a "safe" place both emotionally and intellectually, but it is at the expense of civility and democratic outcomes for learning spaces that value multiple outlooks. These students' responsibility in intellectual pursuits remains individual and while their own learning advances, a community of critical learners with a commitment to civil communication is lost.

There are clues that instructors and their students are spending too much time on one side or the other of the dilemma map. In the dilemma map, instructors who value only high participation of their students risk losing the benefits of the witnessing side of the dilemma: reflection of other perspectives, empathy and humility in intellectual progress, and open-mindedness and the courage to engage with alternative viewpoints. Participants may speak often and share values and opinions, but those opinions may not be infused with perspectival thinking from divergent paradigms leading to egocentric speech and indifference toward other people's experiences. A behavior that might signal an over-reliance on participation is if students' expressions become either egocentric or uniformed by the readings or other students' opinions. Or, if students monopolize conversations and other students appear hesitant to enter the discussion, an instructor should "tune-into" the possibility of over-relying on participation.

There are also clues that instructors and students have over-relied on the witnessing side of the dilemma. If large numbers of students are not participating in the group discussions, the witnessing side of the dilemma may be over-emphasized. Instructors who over emphasize reflection as part of the discussion lose valuable outcomes in discussion instruction. If students seem apathetic toward topics or appear to reflect, but not participate, this negative quadrant of this side of the dilemma map is highlighted in unproductive ways. Additionally, if students are irritated with classroom speech, but only express that irritation after class or within small groups of students not connected with the discussion, the reflection polarity has descended into the lower quadrant of the map. There are clues that instructors and their students are spending too much time on one side or the other of the dilemma map. Table 1.1 provides those clues to instructors on the dilemma between participating and witnessing within discussion.

When instructors are unaware of dilemmas in instruction, they may focus on only one side of the map, unconsciously limiting the outcomes. In the dilemma map, teachers who value participation in discussions may be inflexible toward students who prefer a witnessing modality in discussions, thus marginalizing the significance of reflection, empathy, and intellectual courage in the process of dialogue. Alternatively, instructors who only value the witnessing side of discussion risk losing the input of students who demonstrate intellectual integrity and display a responsibility toward sharing their perspectives within discussion instruction, leading to more democratic pedagogical spaces.

TABLE 1.1   Clues That Instructors Have Over-Relied on Either Participating or Witnessing

Participating	Witnessing
1. Students actively engage, but the dialogue is overly ego-centric, or uniformed by the readings or other students' opinions.	1. Students do not actively engage and are silent during discussions.
2. Students' dialogue seems indifferent or un-empathetic to the experiences of others.	2. Students appear irritated by others' perspectives outside of class or in small group gossip sessions because they disagree with the perspectives produced in dialogue but have not publically stated so.
3. Students engage in soft violence within dialogue by bullying or teasing people or perspectives or by monopolizing which perspectives are heard in discussions.	3. Students are unwilling or unable to move to action. They appear to be caught in constant reflection or indecisiveness.
4. Students appear unwilling to compromise within speech.	4. Reflection and witnessing leads to apathy about the issues.

These clues help the instructor to move from the lower quadrants of this dilemma to the upper quadrant. For example, when the negative quadrant of participating as an outcome is being expressed too frequently, the instructor recognizes the need to move to the witnessing quadrant in instructional choices. In the dilemma map, clues that the lower quadrant is being focused upon requires that the instructor move in a diagonal motion across to the upper quadrant where the positive outcomes of the dilemma may be addressed. Once behaviors are being expressed in the positive quadrant of the opposite side of the dilemma, move to the adjacent positive side to express both upper quadrants of the dilemma in the discussion, making the entire pedagogy more integral and complete. The map in Figure 1.2 demonstrates this conscious instructional choice from negative to positive quadrants.

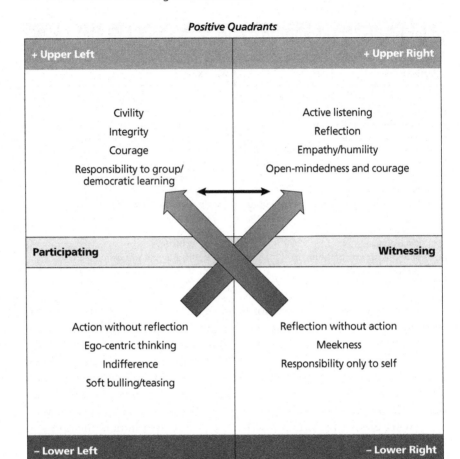

Positive Quadrants

+ Upper Left

Civility

Integrity

Courage

Responsibility to group/
democratic learning

+ Upper Right

Active listening

Reflection

Empathy/humility

Open-mindedness and courage

Participating

Witnessing

Action without reflection

Ego-centric thinking

Indifference

Soft bulling/teasing

Reflection without action

Meekness

Responsibility only to self

– Lower Left

– Lower Right

Negative Quadrants

Figure 1.2   Moving to the positive quadrants.

Summary and Questions

Instructors may find value in both participating and witnessing choices in discussion pedagogy. Both sides of the dilemma have positive outcomes; yet instructors must also be aware of and guard against the negative expressions of the instructional choice. Questions to ask within this dilemma are:

1. What are the benefits of students being encouraged to take a stand and voice their values and opinions in discussion? What are the benefits of active reflection during discussion?

2. What are the benefits of a shared responsibility to group learning by participating? How can humility and courage make for better discussion?
3. How can disinterest in other perspectives threaten productive discussion aimed at civil discourse? How can meekness on the part of a reflective student discourage civil discourse and democratic learning spaces?

2

Democracy and Safety in Discussions

This chapter deals with the interconnected goals of democracy and classroom safety as reciprocal outcomes within discussion pedagogy. Instructors hope that discussions will promote democratic ideals, such as the ability to actually hear and integrate others' perspectives and thoughts into group problem solving. Yet, instructors also want to create a safe climate for their classrooms, where students do not feel under attack and where students do not feel silenced by the opinions of their fellow students. These goals are interdependent within discussions and must be reciprocally valued. A dilemma map demonstrates the positives and negatives of both sides of the dilemma. In addition, clues when an instructor is over-relying on one side of the map are provided and a final visual demonstrates the movement from the lower quadrant to the appropriate upper quadrant when an instructor notices negative behaviors from the lower quadrants. The chapter ends with questions for discussion regarding democracy and safety as mutual goals.

10 Dilemmas in Teaching with Discussion, pages 9–15
Copyright © 2016 by Information Age Publishing
All rights of reproduction in any form reserved.

Dilemma Map of Democracy and Safety in Discussion

Democracy and safety within discussions are mapped in Figure 2.1. In the upper left quadrant, the positive benefits of democracy are listed. In the upper right quadrant, the positive benefits of safety in discussions are given. In the lower left quadrant are the negative consequences of relying solely on democracy as a goal is demonstrated and in the lower right quadrant, the negative consequences of just safety in discussions are provided.

In the upper left quadrant of this dilemma map, the democratic benefits of discussion are listed. For this dilemma map, I rely upon Hess & McAvoy's (2014) research and discussion of the political classroom. A positive

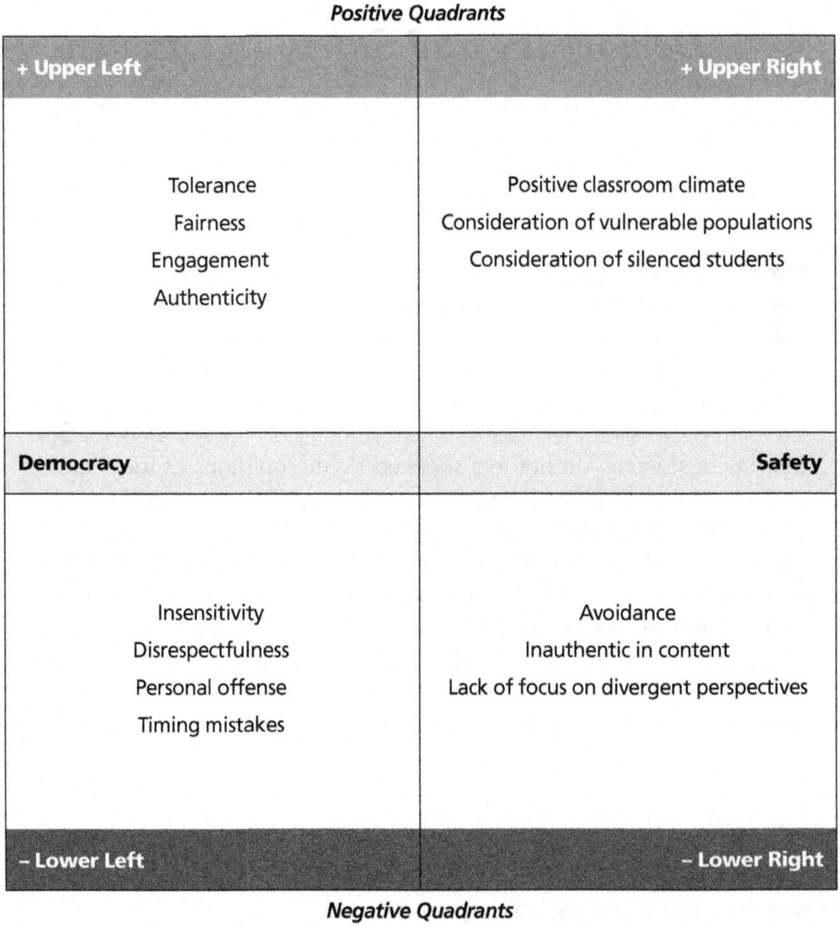

Positive Quadrants

+ Upper Left	+ Upper Right
Tolerance Fairness Engagement Authenticity	Positive classroom climate Consideration of vulnerable populations Consideration of silenced students
Democracy	**Safety**
Insensitivity Disrespectfulness Personal offense Timing mistakes	Avoidance Inauthentic in content Lack of focus on divergent perspectives
– Lower Left	– Lower Right

Negative Quadrants

Figure 2.1 Dilemma map of democracy and safety.

element of democracy as an outcome of discussion is linking discussion to the group decision-making found in public democracies that are promoting the same dispositions in discussions that citizens need in a civil society. Hess & McAvoy (2014) suggested that tolerance, fairness, and political engagement are each critical for creating discussions with democratic intentions. Discussions "increase the variety and frequency of interaction among students who are culturally, linguistically, and racially different from each other" (Parker, 2005, p. 348). Democracies require respect for those whose religious, political, cultural, and ethical views are divergent from the views of other students, and this respect demonstrates the political notion of tolerance. Secondly, discussions promote democratic principles when they expect participants to display fairness. Fairness requires that all students enter a discussion with the purpose of purposely listening to varying perspectives, consider those perspectives from the viewpoints of those who gave them, and commonly find solutions for the issue under discussion. Engagement with controversies in discussion increases students' awareness of and commitment with deliberation, resulting in democratic principles developing as a result of deliberative discussions (Hess & McAvoy, 2014). Last, authenticity is a positive outcome of focusing on democratic discussions. When instructors use authentic questions to guide their discussions, their classrooms become genuinely democratic learning spaces. Deliberation as a principle, allowing the controversy itself to become infused in the content of the lesson despite its sensitive nature, is linked to the goals of tolerance, fairness, and engagement (Hess & McAvoy, 2014).

A focus on the upper right quadrant of the dilemma map reveals the positive outcomes of balancing safety in classroom climate for vulnerable or silenced groups of people as an outcome of discussion. Classroom climate includes the culture, the social relationships, and the individual behaviors of students within the class. Instructors hope their classroom climates are positive and that students feel comfortable and safe. However, some students may become very uncomfortable with some of the sensitive issues inherent in authentic discussions. Additionally, some students are silenced because of personal attributes such as shyness or because they are members of groups who have been historically marginalized in society. Those instructors who choose safety in the dilemma believe that a positive atmosphere can be achieved through creating and establishing group norms of behavior for discussion, and that there are times when controversial issues should be avoided.

The lower left quadrant represents the negative outcomes of focusing solely on democracy as a goal in discussion. Though discussions are authentic and reflect genuine concerns of the students and society, without a value for student safety and a positive classroom climate through agreed upon norms of behavior students in discussions may become insensitive to the experiences of others in their expressions, and these expressions may be interpreted as disrespectful by other students who take personal offense to the attitudes being expressed in deliberations. Democratic learning spaces require an additional focus on civility as part of discourse. Moreover, timing is an issue in this dilemma and being aware of when and how to address controversial issues, so that instructors do not introduce topics at awkward or inappropriate times in their classrooms or before students are developmentally ready, is a potential negative consequence of democracy-oriented discussions.

The lower right quadrant represents the negative possibilities of valuing only safety as an outcome of discussion. Instructors may create discussions that do not deal with highly controversial issues so that students are not placed in a situation where they will need to defend themselves or their choices (Hess & McAvoy, 2014). Though classroom climate may be positive and students do not feel threatened by controversial topics through avoidance of those issues, without genuine discussion of pertinent issues in discussion students may not learn how to engage in civil discussions, a necessary skill for democracy. Hess & McAvoy (2014) suggest that schools are still the most likely venue for students to learn to struggle with controversial issues. Avoidance of those issues for reasons of safety may be at the cost of democracy as a value in education.

There are clues that instructors and their students are spending too much time on one side or the other of the dilemma map. In the dilemma map, instructors who value only democracy of their students risk losing the benefits of the safety side of the dilemma—the importance of a positive climate in classrooms and consideration of vulnerable and silenced students. Instructors who over emphasize democracy as a goal of the discussion lose these valuable outcomes in discussion instruction.

There are also clues that instructors and students have over-relied on safety. Participants may speak in discussions which lack controversy and that do not address sensitive subjects. However, these discussions may lack authenticity for participants when issues of interest to both students and society are avoided. Avoidance of these provocative issues threatens the democratic experience of hearing and responding to opinions divergent from one's own perspectives. These clues are provided in Table 2.1 for democracy and safety within discussion.

When instructors are unaware of dilemmas in instruction, they may focus on only one side of the map, unconsciously limiting the goals and outcomes. In the dilemma map, teachers who value democracy in discussions may be inflexible toward students who are silent or feel threatened by

TABLE 2.1   Clues That Instructors Have Over-Relied on Either Democracy or Safety

Democracy	Safety
1. Student speech appears genuine; however, there seems to be indifference to silent students or to the opinions of vulnerable people in the class.	1. Discussions avoid any controversy.
2. Silent students appear to take offense at how speech is used in the discussion or do not seem to want to risk verbalizing their opinions.	2. Topics of discussion that do arise seem inauthentic or do not garner student interest.
3. An instructor addresses an issue too early in the semester, before a positive classroom climate has been created or before students are developmentally prepared.	3. Students feel safe and there is no risk of potentially troubling topics; however, students do not learn ways to deal with divergent perspectives or learn through civil discourse.
4. Group social norms for ways to address controversial content are not displayed or expected by the instructor.	

conflictual issues, thus marginalizing the value of safety in their classroom climate. Alternatively, instructors who over-value safety as a goal of discussion marginalize the significance of fairness, tolerance, and engagement as democratic principles in classrooms. Instructors who only value safety risk losing those instructional dynamics that result in more democratic pedagogical spaces.

These clues help the instructor to move from the lower quadrants of this dilemma to the upper quadrant. For example, when the negative quadrant of democracy as an outcome is being expressed too much, the instructor knows to move to safety instructional choices. In the dilemma map, clues that the negative expressions of the lower quadrant is being focused upon requires that the instructor move a diagonal motion across to the upper quadrant where the positive outcomes of the dilemma may be addressed. Once behaviors are being expressed in the positive quadrant of the opposite side of the dilemma, move to the adjacent positive side to express both upper quadrants of the dilemma in the discussion, making the entire pedagogy more integral and complete. The map in Figure 2.2 demonstrates this conscious instructional choice from negative to positive quadrants.

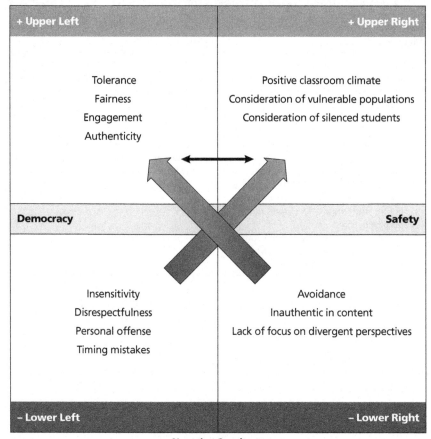

Figure 2.2 Moving to the positive quadrants.

Summary and Questions

Instructors may find value in both democracy and safety choices in discussion pedagogy. Both sides of the dilemma have positive outcomes, yet instructors must also be aware of, and guard against, the negative expressions of the instructional choice. Questions for instructors and their students within this dilemma are:

1. What are the benefits of students being encouraged to actively engage with difficult issues in discussion? What are the benefits of creating a safe classroom climate?

2. Why is civil discourse a benefit of a learning aimed at democracy? How can fairness, tolerance, and engagement make for better discussion? How can focusing solely on democracy threaten productive discussions?
3. What are the benefits of acknowledging silent or vulnerable students? How can focusing solely on safety threaten productive discussion?

3

Structured and Unstructured Discussions

A common instructional dilemma that instructors face with discussion is whether to use a fully structured discussion or to use a more unstructured dynamic. Structure prepares students for consistent expectations. Unstructured discussion is more agile in process and outcomes. There are benefits to both instructional choices. Yet they are interdependent poles as well. Over-reliance on either side of the instructional dilemma can result in negative consequences for discussion.

Dilemma Map of Structured and Unstructured Choices in Discussion

In Figure 3.1, the dilemma between structured and unstructured discussions is mapped. In the upper left quadrant, the positive benefits of using structured discussions are listed. In the upper right quadrant, the positive benefits of using unstructured discussions are given. In the lower left quadrant are the negative consequences of using structure in discussions. In

10 Dilemmas in Teaching with Discussion, pages 17–23
Copyright © 2016 by Information Age Publishing
All rights of reproduction in any form reserved.

Positive Quadrants

+ Upper Left	+ Upper Right
Predictable content Consistency in discussion expectations Predictability of timing in discussions Teacher (or teacher/student)-oriented	Organic flow of content Flexibility in discussion expectations Agility in time choices Student-oriented
Structured Discussions	**Unstructured Discussions**
Rigidity in content Inflexibility in discussion expectations Unbending time expectations Teacher-dominated	Ambiguity in content outcomes Vague discussion expectations Unclear time expectations Student dominated
– Lower Left	– Lower Right

Negative Quadrants

Figure 3.1   Dilemma map of structured and unstructured discussions.

the lower right quadrant, the negative consequences of using unstructured discussions are provided.

In the upper left quadrant of this dilemma map, the benefits of using structured discussions are listed. For example, when the content is predictable through instructor or instructor guided planning, assigned common readings, and clear essential questions, the discussion outcomes are also predictable: common content and common guiding questions, leading to student engagement that centers on those collective curricular goals. When students understand expectations that have been clearly designed by their instructors or by guidelines that they have created, they know that they are required to dialogue and listen; to put forth opinions based upon the readings and also to listen; to be true to their values, be open-minded to others' opinions, and to other product/process outcomes. Focusing on expected timing issues in discussions—such as using a timer in jigsaw activities or planning time for both dominant and quiet students to give input through pairing activities—allow breadth of coverage, a diverse representation of individuals within the group, and space for both communal and individual expressions.

A focus on the upper right quadrant, the positives of unstructured discussions, suggests that organic choices that emerge from student interest, rather than a predetermined structure for content and process, have benefits too. Allowing students to flexibly guide discussions through their own interests and in their own time frame, rather than in a structured manner, results in natural and spontaneous expressions of opinions within discussion. Outcomes are less predictable and deliberate, but the effect may be one that the instructor had not imagined possible, with creativity, fluidity, and an emergent nature unfound in more structured discourse.

The lower left quadrant represents the negative possibilities of structured discussions: rigidity—such that all content is teacher-controlled rather than student-controlled; an inflexibility to the discussion rules, expectations, and guidelines leading to a monotonous or overly controlled process with little spontaneity; and a strictness of time expectations, perhaps by moving students away from undiscussed material before they have mastered it, or before their interests suggest a natural change, or before all students have input into the discussion.

The lower right quadrants represents the negative possibilities of unstructured discussions, such as so much ambiguity in outcomes that students come unprepared or are unable to provide a scholarly basis for their opinions, resulting in uninformed discussion expressions or monologues of individual and non-relational thought. Another negative possibility of this quadrant is that students have so little understanding of the expectations that one or a few students dominate the dialogue, since they do not understand that they should listen as well as speak, or that certain discourses have more power in society than others, resulting in little initiative to actively listen to and engage with alternative perspectives. Similarly, unclear time expectations provide no distinct indicator when the discussion should move to another topic or to another form of the discussion, such as from a whole group to a partner discussion, to encourage collective participation by all students.

There are clues that instructors and their students are spending too much time on one side or the other of the dilemma map. The negative possibilities of using structured discussions may appear when instructors notice when students appear bored or when discussion groups no longer function well because students are not engaged with their assigned roles or because one student is dominating the small group activities. These behaviors may signify students are no longer engaged in the structure of the discussion or that too much time has been spent on a topic or activity. Or students may appear irritated or angry when instructors move to new material or change the topic of discussion. Such behaviors may suggest that the instructor has over-relied on time constraints and structure, and students are not ready to engage with new content because they have not mastered the content and are unprepared for new content.

There are also clues that instructors and students have over-relied on the unstructured discussion. For example, students may appear unengaged in whole class discussions because little facilitation is occurring, and the topic has become mundane or no longer engaging. Or perhaps one or a few students may be dominating the discussion, and when there is little instructor facilitation, the other students are no longer actively involved or are informally rebelling against a classmate who is dominating a too unstructured discussion format. Instructors who have over-relied on unstructured discussions may notice small group discussions are not completing tasks in a timely way or appear unsure of their roles or performance outcomes. Additionally, instructors are unable to achieve a common content discussion because students have not read common previous course readings and are unable to discuss with a shared sense of scholarship as it applies to the discussion at hand. Table 3.1 provides clues to instructors on the dilemma between structured and unstructured choices in discussion.

When instructors are unaware of dilemmas in instruction, they may focus on only one side of the map, unconsciously limiting the outcomes. In the dilemma map, teachers who value structured discussions may be inflexible in their expectations of student choices on topics for dialogue, or may be rigid in their expectations because they lack the awareness of organic and less structured discussion outcomes. Alternatively, instructors who value student voice and input into the topic of discussion may lack the necessary structure for students to engage with common course materials or to accomplish common goals.

These clues help the instructor to move from the lower quadrants of this dilemma to the upper quadrant. For example, when the negative quadrant of structured discussions is being expressed, the instructor knows to move to unstructured choices for discussion. In the dilemma map, clues that the lower quadrant is being focused upon requires that the instructor move in a diagonal motion across to the upper quadrant where the positive

TABLE 3.1 Clues That Instructors Have Over-Relied on Either Structured or Unstructured Choices in Discussion	
Structured Discussions	**Unstructured Discussions**
1. Students appear unengaged in discussion because of lack of interest in the teacher-dominated content and instructional choices. 2. Students complain about roles in small groups because there are no tasks to meet their learning styles, preferences or content interests. 3. Students appear angry or irritated that the instructor has suggested progressing to new content or moving to a new activity because their understanding of the current issues is lacking or because they do not hold great interest in the current issues.	1. One or a few students are dominating both large and small group discussions because there is a lack of focus on student roles in both forms of the discussion. 2. Students are unable to discuss common readings, as they apply to the topic under discussion, or make connections between student dialogues because of a lack of shared content or prior common readings. 3. Students appear unsure of their tasks or outcomes. 4. Students are not completing goals.

outcomes of the dilemma may be addressed. Once behaviors are being expressed in the positive quadrant of the opposite side of the dilemma, move to the adjacent positive side to express both upper quadrants of the dilemma in the discussion, making the entire pedagogy more integral and complete. The map in Figure 3.2 demonstrates this conscious instructional choice from negative to positive quadrants.

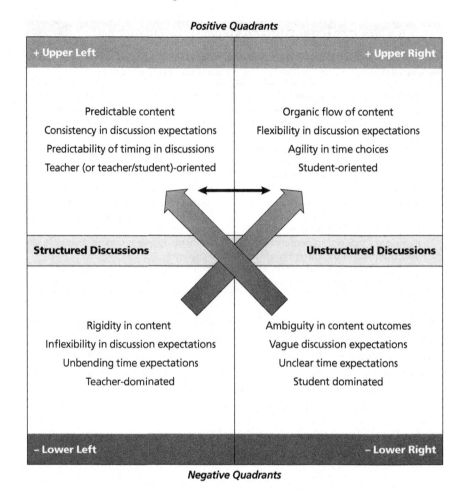

Figure 3.2   Moving to the positive quadrants.

Summary and Questions

Instructors may find value in both structured and unstructured instructional choices in discussion pedagogy. Both sides of the dilemma have positive outcomes; yet, instructors must also be aware of and guard against the negative expressions of the instructional choice. Questions to ask within this dilemma are:

1. What are the benefits of structuring and focusing a topic for discussion? What are the benefits of allowing students to determine the

focus of the discussion content and when to shift to another topic in discussion?

2. How does shared content reading for all students prior to a discussion promote learning? How might an instructor promote personal experience within discussion?

3. Why does structure benefit discussions? When might students best decide the form of discussion (whole group, small group, Socratic seminar, jigsaw groups, etc.)?

4

Scholarliness and Personal Experience in Discussions

This chapter deals with the interconnected goals of scholarliness and personal experience as reciprocal outcomes within discussion pedagogy. Scholarliness means using common course readings or other course content as a reference point to make reasoned and informed decisions within discussion to guard against distorted opinions that rest solely on participants' self-referential viewpoints and fallacious assumptions. However, instructors also want to encourage personal experience as a basis for discussion, especially from students whose experience informs the dialogue from marginalized perspectives. These goals are interdependent within discussions and must be reciprocally valued. A dilemma map demonstrates the positives and negatives of both sides of the dilemma. In addition, clues when an instructor is over-relying on one side of the map are provided, and a final visual demonstrates the movement from the lower quadrant to the appropriate upper quadrant when an instructor notices negative behaviors from the lower quadrants. The chapter ends with questions for discussion regarding scholarliness and personal experience as mutual goals.

10 Dilemmas in Teaching with Discussion, pages 25–31
Copyright © 2016 by Information Age Publishing
All rights of reproduction in any form reserved.

Dilemma Map of Scholarliness and Personal Experience in Discussion

Scholarliness and personal experience within discussions are mapped in Figure 4.1. In the upper left quadrant, the positive benefits of scholarliness are listed. In the upper right quadrant, the positive benefits of personal experience in discussions are given. In the lower left quadrant, the negative consequences of relying solely on scholarliness as a goal are demonstrated, and in the lower right quadrant, the negative consequences of relying only on personal experiences in discussions are provided.

Positive Quadrants

+ Upper Left	+ Upper Right
Logical-scientific reality construction	Subjective or inter-subjective/emic realities
Textually based dialogue	Lived experience through narrative
Pre-discussion preparation	Particularity
Reasoned discourse	Marginalized paradigms are valued
Decisions based on using verified information	Personal and perspectival ways of knowing
Scholarliness	**Personal Experience**
Limitations on reason/rationality	Subjective/ego-centric perspectives
Loss of personal voice	No validation or verification
Dominant paradigms are over-represented	No common materials for students
– Lower Left	– Lower Right

Negative Quadrants

Figure 4.1 Dilemma map of scholarliness and personal experience.

In the upper left quadrant of this dilemma map, the scholarly benefits of discussion are listed. A positive element of requiring scholarliness in discussions is the academic focus of using common outside texts for students with which to engage prior to class; thus promoting dialogue based in academic knowledge. Classroom talk based in research or theory may result in more reasoned discourse with a focus on truth-seeking and a disposition of analytical contemplation (Facione, 2000). With the intention of creating discussions grounded in a common text (which is loosely interpreted to mean written, visual, or audio materials), Socratic style discussions require students to prepare for discussion prior to class (Roberts & Billings, 1999) through reading (or viewing or hearing) materials related to the topic, and pre-preparing by addressing questions about the text or creating other graphic organizers, such as a the Three R's—reading, reacting, and responding (Anderson & Piro, in press a). Toward the goal of textually informed dialogue and reasoned discourse, Adler (1998) termed "enlarged understandings," as an aim of instruction through the application of content and reading to open-ended questions. Similarly, Parker and Hess (2001) suggested referring to the text prior to discussion with a question such as, "What does the author mean?" (p. 281) This requirement focuses on a disposition of scholarliness and use of text to inform the participant's dialogue in discussion. Referring to perspectives based in common text, participants explore guiding questions in a manner that relocates their dialogue to include and consider authors' or artists' understandings of issues. When students make decisions, their interpretations are based upon verified data.

In the upper right quadrant of this dilemma map, the personal experience benefits of discussion are listed. Discussion incorporates the participant's lived experiences as they intersect with the issue at hand. Even Socrates did not always play the devil's advocate but used his own life as a personal example in discussion (Sullivan, Smith, & Matusov, 2009). Humans organize their experience in the form of narrative—of personal stories drawn from encounters with the world and with their own subjective knowledge (Bruner, 1991). When that experience includes feeling silenced by dominant societal discourses—such as when women produce knowledge in different ways than through male-dominated processes (Blenkey, et al., 1986) or through prevailing political, cultural, or ethnic frameworks (Freire, 1993; hooks, 1989) that are marginalized by dominant paradigms and white supremacy, or when knowledge feels vintriloquic in that it has been handed down by others but not experienced by the self (Kelly, 1997)—personal experiences may clash with official knowledge. This quadrant of the dilemma map is where the positive outcomes of valuing personal and marginalized experience in discussion can be discovered. This quadrant relies on the notion of knowledge creation as accretive, starting with particulars that may eventually lead to general and universal knowledge. These particular instances and subjective examples of experiences which are cultural, gendered, personal, and subjective and which may be distinct from official academic knowledge are produced within discussion when this side of the dilemma map is valued. In this quadrant, knowledge production is viewed as a contextual dialogic between people and their world.

The lower left quadrant represents the negative outcomes of focusing solely on scholarliness as a goal in discussion. Though discussions rely on academic and scholarly text in this side of the dilemma, reasoned and scientific texts may be viewed as a Western and scientific mode of knowledge production grounded in Enlightenment philosophy that lacks those perspectives which are not found in these traditions, including subjective and inter-subjective knowledge. Exclusive use of research-based texts for the disposition of scholarliness may result in the loss of an emic approach to knowledge—the personal and subjective experiences of students as they relate to the topic under discussion—and may not acknowledge the ways that power intersects with official knowledge and works to exclude those marginalized discourses that may be found in personal experiences to recognize only those discourses that have power in society (Foucault, 1980).

The lower right quadrant represents the negative possibilities of valuing only personal voice as an outcome of discussion. Instructors may create discussions that enhance and embrace individual students' experiences as they connect with the topic of discussion. However, an over-use of this side of the dilemma may result in merely individual, personal, subjective, and egocentric expressions that are deficient in outside knowledge referents. When students lack a common reading or textual reference, the only orientation is self-referential, and discussion becomes unconnected to outside knowledge or perspectives. The community building experiences of working with common texts are absent from the dialogue. Additionally, with an exclusive focus on personal experience in discussion, verification and validation of those experiences as they relate to outside textual authorities is absent.

There are clues that instructors and their students are spending too much time on one side or the other of the dilemma map. In the dilemma map, instructors who value only scholarliness risk losing the benefits of the personal experience—the importance of subjective knowledge and insider perspectives. Instructors who overemphasize scholarliness as a goal of the discussion lose these valuable outcomes in discussion instruction. Instructors may observe for behaviors—such as no references to personal experience in the discussion, an inability to connect the text with larger human perspectives, or an exclusive use of reason and rationality for decision-making—to suggest that they have over-relied on scholarliness in their instructional expectations.

There are also clues that instructors and students have over-emphasized personal experience as a goal. Participants may provide their personal experiences in discussions but lose the communal understandings that come when using a common text for group discussions, connecting the issue and student experiences to outside authorities and knowledge bound in reason and rationality. Clues that the instructor has over-relied on personal experiences are behaviors such as student comments that are self-referential only and which lack the perspectives of outside research and theory. These clues are provided in Table 4.1 for scholarliness and personal experience within discussion.

When instructors are unaware of dilemmas in instruction, they may focus on only one side of the map, unconsciously limiting the outcomes. In the dilemma map, teachers who value scholarliness in discussions may be inflexible toward students who express personal experiences as they relate to the topic of discussion, thus marginalizing the significance of subjective, cultural, ethnic, gendered, and emerging knowledge. Alternatively, instructors who only value personal experience miss important opportunities for students to engage with outside collective readings that connect the students in the class and the topic of issue to larger contexts beyond the personal.

These clues help the instructor to move from the lower quadrants of this dilemma to the upper quadrants. For example, when the negative quadrant of scholarliness as an outcome is being expressed too much, the

TABLE 4.1   Clues that Instructors Have Over-Relied on Either Scholarliness or Personal Experience

Scholarliness	Personal Experience
1. Students who have experiences related to the topic are unwilling to share those experiences with the class because they are not grounded in the common texts that are assigned. 2. Students discussions are based in readings and scientific knowledge, but students are unable to translate that knowledge to their own personal paradigms and life experiences. 3. Expressions of personal experience by students are marginalized because they do not match official knowledge.	1. Students express personal opinions from experience but are unable to connect that experience to larger perspectives, knowledge or human experiences. 2. Students' expressions are self-referential and discrete. 3. Students are unable to interact with each other outside of personal accounts because there were not assigned common readings or other textual materials used for the discussion.

instructor knows to move to personal experience instructional choices. In the dilemma map, clues that the lower quadrant is being focused upon requires that the instructor move in a diagonal motion across to the upper quadrant where the positive outcomes of the dilemma may be addressed. Once behaviors are being expressed in the positive quadrant of the opposite side of the dilemma, move to the adjacent positive side to express both upper quadrants of the dilemma in the discussion, making the entire pedagogy more integral and complete. The map in Figure 4.2 demonstrates this conscious instructional choice from negative to positive quadrants.

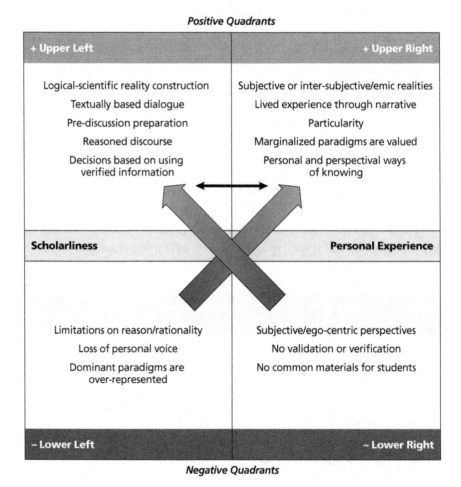

Positive Quadrants

+ Upper Left	+ Upper Right
Logical-scientific reality construction	Subjective or inter-subjective/emic realities
Textually based dialogue	Lived experience through narrative
Pre-discussion preparation	Particularity
Reasoned discourse	Marginalized paradigms are valued
Decisions based on using verified information	Personal and perspectival ways of knowing
Scholarliness	**Personal Experience**
Limitations on reason/rationality	Subjective/ego-centric perspectives
Loss of personal voice	No validation or verification
Dominant paradigms are over-represented	No common materials for students
– Lower Left	– Lower Right

Negative Quadrants

Figure 4.2 Moving to the positive quadrants.

Summary and Questions

Instructors may find value in both scholarly and personal experience choices in discussion pedagogy. Both sides of the dilemma have positive outcomes; yet instructors must also be aware of and guard against the negative expressions of the instructional choice. Questions for instructors and their students within this dilemma are:

1. What are the benefits of students actively engaging with common texts prior to and during discussion? What are the benefits of personal experience?
2. How can reasoned discourse improve discussion? How can personal experience be marginalized when scholarliness alone is valued?
3. Why is personal experience a valuable companion to traditional textual knowledge for discussions? Why can focusing solely on personal experience threaten productive discussion?

5

Cognitive and Social/Emotional Learning

This chapter deals with the interconnected goals of both cognitive and social/emotional learning within discussion pedagogy. Instructors want students to create cognitive learning from discussions. Traditional learning outcomes emphasize various forms of cognitive learning, such as problem-solving, convergent and divergent thinking, critical thinking, creative thinking, and higher-order thinking. Instructors hope that the outcome of discussion will yield these cognitive thinking skills. Yet, instructors also want students to display compassion, self and other understanding, ethical thought processes and actions, and conflict resolution, or what Daniel Goleman (2006) and the Collaborative for Academic, Social, and Emotional Learning (CASEL) would define as social and emotional learning. These goals are interdependent within discussions and must be reciprocally valued. In fact, problem solving, critical thinking, and other cognitive processes are enhanced through engagement with the emotional part of the brain (Goleman, 2006). A dilemma map demonstrates the positives and negatives of both sides of the dilemma. In addition, clues when

10 Dilemmas in Teaching with Discussion, pages 33–40
Copyright © 2016 by Information Age Publishing
All rights of reproduction in any form reserved.

an instructor is over-relying on one side of the map are provided and a final visual demonstrates the movement from the lower quadrant to the appropriate upper quadrant when an instructor notices negative behaviors from the lower quadrants. The chapter ends with questions for discussion regarding cognitive and social/emotional learning as mutual goals.

Dilemma Map of Cognitive Learning and Social/Emotional Learning in Discussion

Cognitive and social/emotional learning within discussions are mapped in Figure 5.1. In the upper left quadrant, the positive benefits of cognitive learning are listed. In the upper right quadrant, the positive benefits of social/emotional learning in discussions are given. In the lower left quadrant are the negative consequences of using only cognitive learning, and in the lower right quadrant, the negative consequences of social/emotional in discussions are provided.

In the upper left quadrant of this dilemma map, the cognitive learning benefits of discussion are listed. A positive element of cognitive learning in discussion is that it aligns with what might be viewed as traditional academic learning outcomes for education. Cognitive learning (or learning in the cognitive domain, see Bloom et al., 1956) may be classified as simple or complex (Gagne & Berliner, 1984); analytical, creative, and practice-based (Sternberg, 1985); componential, experiential, and contextual (Sternberg, cited in Crowl, Kaminsky, & Podell, 1997); logic and reasoning, analyzing, and reading and writing (Dunn, Dunn, & Price, 1977); within dimensions of learning (Marzano, et al., 1988); or declarative, procedural, and conditional knowledge (Jacobs & Paris, 1987; Schraw & Moshman, 1995; Shulman, 1986, 1987). These forms of skills and knowledge support various forms of assessments required in educational contexts, such as standardized and teacher-created tests, essays and oral performances, and performance based assessments. Cognitive learning includes the academic skills and knowledge that educators have customarily promoted within their classrooms: memory skills; interpretation; classifying; summarizing; inferring; comparing; organizing; planning; convergent and divergent thinking; comprehension, application, and evaluation skills; meta-cognition; scientific inquiry; and problem-solving. Discussions can scaffold and support cognitive learning and assessments.

Positive Quadrants

+ Upper Left	+ Upper Right
Academic skills and knowledge Critical thinking Divergent/convergent thinking Problem-solving	Reflection Dispositions Empathy and compassion Self/other-awareness Ethics
Cognitive Learning	**Social-Emotional Learning**
All head, no heart Little reflection Pragmatic Low social awareness	Irrational Manipulative Time intensive
– Lower Left	– Lower Right

Negative Quadrants

Figure 5.1 Dilemma map of cognitive and social/emotional learning.

Cognitive learning suggests "good thinking," and as such, critical thinking is also a component of cognitive learning. There are many taxonomies and guidelines for improving critical thinking (Lai, 2011) within cognitive learning. For example, Elder and Paul's (2008) nine universal intellectual standards (Elder & Paul, 2008) are clarity, accuracy, precision, relevance, depth, breadth, logic, significance, and fairness. These standards assess the quality of reasoning about a problem (Elder & Paul, 2007). Furthermore, a taxonomic approach to learning (Bloom et al., 1956) is widely used in education to encourage the higher order thinking skills of synthesis and evaluation.

A focus on the upper right quadrant, the positives of social/emotional learning (SEL), suggests that social and emotional learning within a discussion have value, too. Self-reflection regarding issues within discussion is a significant component of SEL. According to Rodgers,

> Reflection is a meaning-making process that moves a learner from one experience into the next with deeper understanding of its relationships with and connections to other experiences and ideas. It is the thread that makes continuity of learning possible and ensures the progress of the individual and, ultimately, society. It is a means to essentially moral ends. (2002, p. 845)

As a result, reflection needs to occur within community, such as within discussion pedagogy, to acknowledge both personal and group growth.

Additionally, SEL encourages dispositions that support this type of learning and which further support cognitive learning. These "habits of mind" (Meier, 2002), or what Paul (1993) called intellectual traits, encourage the social/emotional learning of this quadrant of the dilemma map. These traits include humility, compassion, open-mindedness, and empathy. Further, SEL upholds critical analysis in that the ability to use critical thinking may be separate from the disposition to think critically (Facione, 1990, 2000). Therefore, if *good* thinking (cognitive learning) "is synonymous with critical thinking, a person who has the ability to think critically but decides not to do so is not a critical thinker" (Lai, 2011, p. 12). Social/emotional learning also fosters fair mindedness—awareness of other's perspectives, struggles, and challenges—as well as metacognition and self-awareness of one's own perspectives. Lastly, social/emotional learning gives rise to an ethical focus resulting in moral knowing, moral feeling, and moral action (Wangaard, n.d.) within discussion instruction. The two sides of the dilemma interrelate in a manner that promotes the other.

The lower left quadrant represents the negative outcomes of focusing solely on students' cognitive learning in discussion. When students only learn cognitively without social/emotional learning in discussions, their perspectives may represent excellent critical thought with little heart or compassion. Furthermore, absent critical reflection of the nature of how power intersects with discourses or within paradigms in culture, problem-solving and analysis may maintain practices bound in oppression and marginalization of people. Concomitantly, cognitive learning that is "good thinking" without social/emotional components of learning may represent pragmatic and reasonable outcomes that are not ethical, moral, nor bound in culturally accepted norms of behavior. Lastly, individuals may produce exceptional instances of cognitive learning, but be unable to communicate or represent that knowledge to others or to consider the application of that learning to the community without a focus on social/emotional outcomes of learning.

The lower right quadrant represents the negative possibilities of only social/emotional learning within discussion pedagogy. Social/emotional learning in discussions may reflect compassionate and interactional dynamics with the class or the outside community, but without the standards of critical analysis, those outcomes may be irrational or may not represent the best practices of a knowledge base. Additionally, social/emotional learning takes a time commitment by instructors and students that may threaten content coverage for other, central standards of a discipline. Last, having high social/emotional intelligence (Goleman, 2006) may result in manipulation of other people (Kilduff, Chiaburu, & Menges, 2010; Menges, Kilduff, Kern, & Bruch, 2015) or an orientation to others' emotions at the cost of noncompletion of important tasks (Joseph & Newman, 2010).

There are clues that instructors and their students are spending too much time on one side or the other of the dilemma map. In the dilemma map, instructors who only value cognitive learning risk losing the benefits of the social/emotional learning side of the dilemma: critical reflection of how power is embedded in discourse; dispositions of communication, empathy and compassion, self-and other awareness and ethical actions. Students may engage in excellent thinking processes and outcomes, but the learning may not be infused with a deep awareness of others and their challenges. A behavior that might signal an over-reliance on cognitive learning is if students' actions or comments appear well-conceived, but lack understanding or compassion. Or, if students value and display only rationality over empathy, an instructor should "tune into" the possibility they have over-relied on cognitive learning.

There are also clues that instructors and students have over-relied on the social/emotional learning side of the dilemma. If students are empathetically communicating in the group discussions, but the outcomes appear irrational or not grounded in the research or best practices of a discipline, the SEL side of the dilemma may be over-emphasized. If students seem to manipulate or use their high social/emotional intelligence to influence others in the class rather than as an outcome of learning and communicating, this negative quadrant of this side of the dilemma map is highlighted in unproductive ways. Finally, if too much time is spent on social/emotional outcomes, important content may be missed when the social/emotional polarity has descended into the lower quadrant of the map.

There are clues that instructors and their students are spending too much time on one side or the other of the dilemma map. Table 5.1 provides

TABLE 5.1   Clues that Instructors Have Over-Relied on Either Cognitive Learning or Social/Emotional Learning

Cognitive	Social/Emotional
1. Students use rational thought processes, but do not appear concerned with how their outcomes affect real people.	1. Students listen and speak with social/ emotional intelligence. However, they seem unconcerned with the irrationality of their comments.
2. Students do not use social/emotional communication. They do not listen well. Their dialogue is combative or brash.	2. Students appear to be manipulating others; their dialogue or actions appear unauthentic and aimed at influencing others.
3. Students are pragmatic but uncompassionate.	3. Students display high social/emotional skills. However the discussions are unwieldy in time.
4. Students' arguments are well-reasoned and bound in best practices. However, they are unable to communicate the results to others in an effective manner.	4. Little content is covered.

those clues to instructors on the dilemma between cognitive learning and social/emotional learning within discussion.

When instructors are unaware of dilemmas in instruction, they may focus on only one side of the map, unconsciously limiting the outcomes. In the dilemma map, teachers who value cognitive learning in discussions may be inflexible toward students who prefer social/emotional learning in discussions, thus marginalizing the significance of reflection, empathy, and ethics in the process of discussion. Alternatively, instructors who only value the social/emotional side of discussion risk losing the input of students who demonstrate excellent critical analysis and problem-solving aptitudes and outcomes.

These clues help the instructor to move from the lower quadrants of this dilemma to the upper quadrant. For example, when the negative quadrant of cognitive learning as an outcome is being expressed too frequently, the instructor recognizes the need to move to the social/emotional quadrant in instructional choices. In the dilemma map, clues that the lower quadrant is being focused upon requires that the instructor move in a diagonal motion across to the upper quadrant where the positive outcomes of the dilemma may be addressed. Once behaviors are being expressed in the positive quadrant of the opposite side of the dilemma, move to the adjacent positive side to express both upper quadrants of the dilemma in the discussion, making the entire pedagogy more integral and complete. The map in Figure 5.2 demonstrates this conscious instructional choice from negative to positive quadrants.

Positive Quadrants

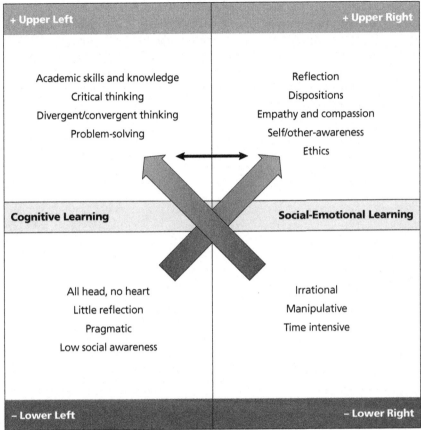

Figure 5.2 Moving to the positive quadrants.

Summary and Questions

Instructors may find value in both cognitive learning and social/emotional learning choices in discussion pedagogy. Both sides of the dilemma have positive outcomes, yet instructors must also be aware of and guard against the negative expressions of the instructional choice. Questions to ask within this dilemma are:

1. What are the benefits of students being encouraged to use varied cognitive learning processes in discussion? What are the benefits of

critical analysis and problem solving during discussion? Why does over-reliance on cognitive learning threaten discussion?

2. What are the benefits of a social/emotional learning in discussions? How can empathy and compassion make for better discussion? Why can disinterest in social/emotional learning threaten productive discussion using rationality? How can manipulation of one's own emotions or others' emotions threaten the authenticity and ethical dimension of discussion?

6

Product and Process in Discussions

This chapter deals with the interconnected goals of product and process as reciprocal effects of discussion pedagogy. Product refers to the individual or group outcomes of instruction which might be written or may be a performance, they may also be graded or ungraded. There is a task orientation toward content development, creation of a product with instructor created guidelines, or results. Process refers to the ongoing people-orientation of discussion which emphasizes the journey itself as the desired consequence. These goals are interdependent within discussions and must be reciprocally valued. A dilemma map demonstrates the positives and negatives of both sides of the dilemma. In addition, clues when an instructor is over-relying on one side of the map are provided and a final visual demonstrates the movement from the lower quadrant to the appropriate upper quadrant when an instructor notices negative behaviors from the lower quadrants. The chapter ends with questions for discussion regarding product and process as mutual goals in discussion.

10 Dilemmas in Teaching with Discussion, pages 41–47
Copyright © 2016 by Information Age Publishing
All rights of reproduction in any form reserved.

Dilemma Map of Product and Process in Discussion

Product and process within discussions are mapped in Figure 6.1. In the upper left quadrant, the positive benefits of product as outcomes are listed. In the upper right quadrant, the positive benefits of process within discussions are given. In the lower left quadrant are the negative consequences of relying solely on product as a goal is demonstrated and in the lower right quadrant, the negative consequences of relying only on process in discussions are provided.

In the upper left quadrant of this dilemma map, the benefits of discussion which rely on product-orientations are listed. Students are provided

Positive Quadrants

+ Upper Left	+ Upper Right
Task/content orientation Individual and group assessments Clear procedures Creation/result Instructor guidelines	People orientation Team process Fluid procedures Formative Journey/activity oriented Student guided
Product	**Process**
Instructor oriented Rigidity Unreasonable Summative only	Group oriented Ambiguous Lack of direction Inadequate learning
– Lower Left	– Lower Right

Negative Quadrants

Figure 6.1 Dilemma map product and process.

individual rubrics or guidelines regarding their expectations within the discussion: participation and listening, considering other perspectives and developing intellectual autonomy, dialoguing and questioning, presentations, and more. These individual or group guidelines are task-oriented; they assist the learner to understand the common expectations of the discussion instruction—what they should produce from the discussion. As such, the product side of the dilemma map represents clarity and consistency about the ways students should engage with others in discussion. This side of the dilemma map suggests that creation or development of an end result—participation within discussion; reading the common literature before class to engage in informed dialogue; or a self-analysis of learning or a group presentation—has clear and specific guidelines toward that product. The product might be the students' own reflection of growth, engagement with the course materials, or movement from little to increased participation or to more questioning. For example, an end product might be heightened use of the varying levels of the intellectual standards with Socratic questions. To scaffold this end product, the instructor might provide a personal checklist for students to monitor the types and frequencies of Socratic questions they, or people on their team, are producing within discussion (Piro & Anderson, 2015). Alternatively, instructors might provide a rubric or typology with discussion elements that students may use to self-monitor throughout the semester (Piro & Anderson, 2016). The end product/result tends to have structure and clear expectations for students to self-regulate their own progress in discussion instruction.

In the upper right quadrant of this dilemma map, the benefits of process in discussion are listed. Instead of a task or product orientation, this side of the dilemma map focuses on process and people and the formative side of assessment. An inclination toward the team—other students in the class—is favored over the end product of the discussion. A benefit of this position is that safety and group awareness are accentuated to encourage participation, other voices, and democratically-oriented engagement between students. How students navigate the process is less structured and there may be few explicit guidelines, taxonomies, or rubrics used, or the rubrics are used for formative purposes only. The journey or the activity of the discussion—the process and engagement within discussion, itself—is the desired outcome.

The lower left quadrant represents the negative outcomes of focusing solely on product as a goal in discussion. Though discussions flourish when individuals and groups of students understand the clear products they are expected to produce, the exclusive use of product orientation does not encourage students to "live in the moment" of the discussion. It inspires them to orient toward instructor expectations rather than their own self-regulation and the natural and organic flow of group processes. Rubrics and taxonomies may become cumbersome in discussions when students attend to them as outcomes rather than as maps toward the outcomes. Product orientations may become unreasonable or unrealistic when discussions evolve into dialogue about student interests that are outside of the instructor's own interests and, as a result, become irrelevant to the expected products. Lastly, the product side focuses only on the summative nature of discussion rather than the formative, continuing, and developing characteristics of student engagement.

The lower right quadrant represents the negative possibilities of valuing only process as an outcome of discussion. Instructors may create discussions that enhance and embrace the group and individual students' voices and perspectives within the group and value the actual process of discussion. However, an over-use of this side of the dilemma may result in an exclusive focus on people orientation, and very little work or product may emerge from the discussion. When students give preference solely to the process of creating and maintaining community and group orientation—the process part of discussion—the discussion may lack the structure, clarity, and end purpose for students to remain engaged, finish a task, or improve their own individual discussion skills. Content learning may not develop as completely without product outcomes and individual skills—such as dialogue and questioning, open-mindedness and autonomy, and scholarliness and personal experience—may remain immature and underdeveloped.

There are clues that instructors and their students are spending too much time on one side or the other of the dilemma map (Table 6.1). In the dilemma map, instructors who value only product outcomes risk losing the benefits of the process itself—the importance of fluidity and other-people orientation for exploring difficult and complex ideas in dialogue. Instructors who over emphasize process as a goal of the discussion also lose valuable outcomes in discussion instruction, such as individual growth of the specified components of effective discussion.

When instructors are unaware of dilemmas in instruction, they may focus on only one side of the map, unconsciously limiting the outcomes. In the dilemma map, teachers who value product outcomes in discussions may be inflexible toward students who express the need for process in discussion, thus marginalizing the significance of group orientation, natural and organic expressions in discussions, and a focus beyond the individual's or groups' products. Alternatively, instructors who only value process miss important opportunities for students to experience content outcomes with clear, instructor informed guidelines.

TABLE 6.1   Clues That Instructors Have Over-Relied on Either Product or Process

Product	Process
1. Students are too focused on the guidelines, rubrics or taxonomies during small or large group discussions and miss important organic information that is suggested within the discussion. 2. Students become overly focused on their individual development at the expense of the group. 3. Students seem overly focused on the outcome of the group but not on the process toward that result. 4. Students are apprehensive about the instructor's expectations for their behaviors in discussion rather than their own self-regulation or the actual process of the discussion, itself.	1. Students miss time deadlines for products. 2. Students express uncertainty about next steps within the discussion. 3. Students are unable to represent sufficient content outcomes after their discussion. 4. Students appear unconcerned with expectations about products. 5. Expressions about honoring the process—such as spending more time on an issue to hear all sides of an argument—are met with groans or eye rolls.

These clues help the instructor to move from the lower quadrants of this dilemma to the upper quadrant. For example, when the negative quadrant of product as an outcome is being expressed too much, the instructor knows to move to process instructional choices. In the dilemma map, clues that the lower quadrant is being focused upon requires that the instructor move in a diagonal motion across to the upper quadrant where the positive outcomes of the dilemma may be addressed. Once behaviors are being expressed in the positive quadrant of the opposite side of the dilemma, move to the adjacent positive side to express both upper quadrants of the dilemma in the discussion, making the entire pedagogy more integral and complete. The map in Figure 6.2 demonstrates this conscious instructional choice from negative to positive quadrants.

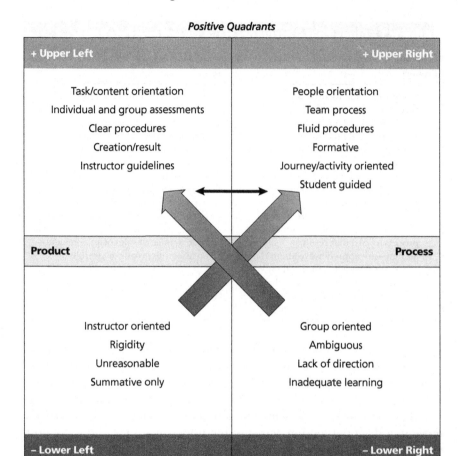

Figure 6.2 Moving to the positive quadrants.

Summary and Questions

Instructors may find value in both product and process choices in discussion pedagogy. Both sides of the dilemma have positive outcomes, yet instructors must also be aware of and guard against the negative expressions of the instructional choice. Questions for instructors and their students within this dilemma are:

1. What are the benefits of students orienting their success through a common product in discussion? What are the benefits of a focus on process?

2. How can discussion be improved with clear guidelines for individual or group performance? How can the product be marginalized when process alone is valued? How can instructor expectations threaten the process side of discussion?
3. Why is process so valuable within a discussion? In what ways can an emphasis on process threaten the creation of products?

7

Relational and Personal Learning

This chapter deals with the interconnected goals of both relational/ social learning and personal/ individual learning in discussion pedagogy. A common instructional dilemma that instructors face with discussion is whether to focus upon learning based on group or individual outcomes. There are benefits to both instructional choices. Yet, they are interdependent outcomes as well. Over-reliance on either pole can create some instructional problems and incomplete pedagogical goals. A dilemma map is demonstrated based on relational and personal learning, a map that was informed by Johnson's (1998) team and individual polarity. In addition, clues when an instructor is over-relying on one side of the map are provided, and a final visual demonstrates the movement from the lower quadrant to the appropriate upper quadrant when an instructor notices negative behaviors from the lower quadrants. The chapter ends with questions for discussion regarding the dilemma.

10 Dilemmas in Teaching with Discussion, pages 49–54
Copyright © 2016 by Information Age Publishing
All rights of reproduction in any form reserved.

Dilemma Map of Relational and Personal Learning in Discussion

In Figure 7.1, relational and personal learning in discussions are mapped. In the upper left quadrant, the positive benefits of using relational discussions are listed. In the upper right quadrant, the positive benefits of using personal learning discussions are given. In the lower left quadrant are the negative consequences of using relational learning in discussions. In the lower right quadrant, the negative consequences of using personal learning in discussions are provided.

Positive Quadrants

+ Upper Left	+ Upper Right
Connectedness Civility in discourse Peer support Complexity of thought	Uniqueness Personal autonomy Individual creativity
Relational Learning	**Personal Learning**
Conformity of thought Group think (herd mentality) Loss of individual creativity	Isolation in learning No focus on civility as an outcome No peer support
– Lower Left	– Lower Right

Negative Quadrants

Figure 7.1 Dilemma map of relational and personal learning.

In the upper left quadrant of this dilemma map, the relational learning benefits of discussion are listed. A positive element of relational learning is the connectedness and sense of belonging that students acquire through an exchange of ideas in a social context. An additional benefit is the ability to dialogue about those difficult and complex issues through respectful but engaging civil discourse, an outcome that is related to democratic pedagogy. Group learning lends itself to complex thinking in that groups may have more capacity than individuals to embrace ambiguous and contradictory perspectives. Last, peer support for learning through prompts, asking for clarification or depth regarding an issue under discussion, or the actual social learning that occurs from interacting with others are all upper left quadrant benefits.

A focus on the upper right quadrant, the positives of personal learning, suggests that individual learning and consciousness about one's own learning and assumptions are valuable for discussion, too. A further benefit is the development of personal autonomy, whereby one clearly understands where he or she stands on issues and is able to use rational discourse to set forth that stance, a skill that may not require a social component to learning. Further, individual creativity unencumbered by group conformity is enhanced through a focus on this quadrant.

The lower left quadrant represents the negative possibilities of relational learning in discussion—the possibility of conformity of thought in group contexts when it becomes the cultural norm to not disagree, or when marginalized discourses are under-valued within a discussion, leading to Group Think (Janis, 1972) or a herd mentality at the expense of individual and metacognitive growth. As well, in a relational learning, only context individual creativity may be lost to conformity to the group.

The lower right quadrant represents the negative possibilities of only individual or personal learning in discussion pedagogy. Intellectual isolation is a good prospect without relational and social learning contexts. As a result of that isolation, it is difficult to build civility and civil discourse as positive outcomes of democratic pedagogy, such as with instruction with discussion. The individual student relies solely on himself or herself for feedback, greatly reducing the possibility of outside perspectives and cognitive dissonance in a closed feedback loop.

There are clues that instructors and their students are spending too much time on one side or the other of the dilemma map. Instructors who value group learning in discussions may be unaware that this discussion format can result in outcomes that lack diversity or creativity as students attempt to work collaboratively because they lack the awareness of the benefits of personal learning in discussions. For example, students may be engaged in group learning but their products may lack creativity and divergence. If conformity to the group becomes the norm, or if students are unable to understand their own vested interests in their problem-solving or products, the relational side of the dilemma map has been over-relied upon.

There are also clues that instructors and students have over-relied on personal learning. Instructors who value only individual learning may emphasize outcomes that are not focused upon civility among perspectives that fall outside of individual opinions. For example, students may work individually and create products that are unique and creative, but those products may lack perspectival thinking and include incomplete or only particular viewpoints. These clues are provided below for relational and personal learning. Table 7.1 provides clues to instructors on the dilemma between structured and unstructured choices in discussion.

These clues help the instructor to move from the lower quadrants of this dilemma to the upper quadrant. For example, when the negative quadrant of relational learning is being expressed, the instructor knows to move to personal learning to support discussion. In the dilemma map, clues that the lower quadrant is being focused upon requires that the instructor move in a diagonal motion across to the upper quadrant where the positive outcomes of the dilemma may be addressed. Once behaviors are being expressed in the positive quadrant of the opposite side of the dilemma, move to the adjacent positive side to express both upper quadrants of the dilemma in the discussion, making the entire pedagogy more integral and

TABLE 7.1 Clues That Instructors Have Over-Relied on Either Relational or Personal Learning	
Relational Learning	**Personal Learning**
1. Creativity seems hindered by a focus on group goals and outcomes. 2. There is little diversity of perspectives because of common thinking between group members. Individual viewpoints are subsumed under group thought. 3. Conformity, rather than divergent perspectives, is valued and, as a result, the group is unable to comprehend their own vested interests or whether they are accurately analyzing outside perspectives. 4. Students express negative comments about group work.	1. The ability to relate to others appears to be constrained to a focus on the individual student's perspectives. 2. Individuals are unable or unwilling to consider perspectives outside of their own ego-centric thinking. 3. Individuals are unable to discuss with principles of civility as they focus solely on their own opinions instead of valuing group dialogue and democratic exchange. 4. Students are unable to work in a team.

complete. The map in Figure 7.2 demonstrates the directional movement of this conscious instructional choice from negative to positive quadrants and the constructive direction of the movement within the map.

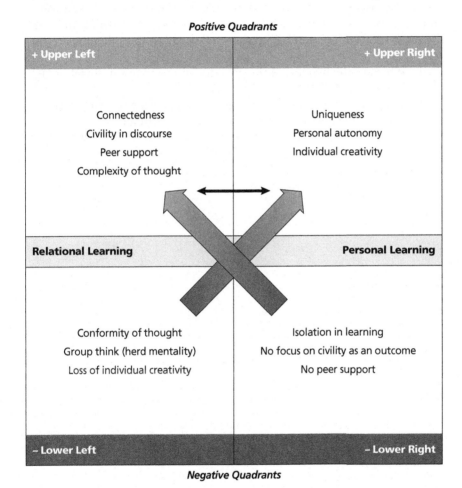

Figure 7.2 Moving to the positive quadrants.

Summary and Questions

Instructors may find value in both relational and personal instructional choices in discussion pedagogy. Both sides of the dilemma have positive outcomes, yet instructors must also be aware of and guard against the negative expressions of the poles. Questions to ask within this dilemma are:

1. What are the benefits of the goal of connectedness in social/relational learning? What are the risks?
2. Why is civility enhanced through relational learning? How can creativity be enhanced through personal learning?
3. Why does Group Think threaten relational learning? How does isolation in learning threaten civility and democratic outcomes for learning?

8

Autonomy and Open-Mindedness in Discussions

This chapter deals with the interconnected goals of intellectual autonomy and open-mindedness as mutual outcomes within discussion pedagogy. Instructors hope that students will develop the ability to have rational confidence in their beliefs, values, and inferences, or what might be termed intellectual autonomy (Paul, 1993), while simultaneously encouraging open-mindedness, or the ability to consider new and differing perspectives (Dewey, 1933; 1944).

These goals are interdependent within discussions and must be reciprocally valued. A dilemma map demonstrates the positives and negatives of both sides of the dilemma. In addition, clues when an instructor is over-relying on one side of the map are provided, and a final visual demonstrates the movement from the lower quadrant to the appropriate upper quadrant when an instructor notices negative behaviors from the lower quadrants. The chapter ends with questions for discussion regarding autonomy and open-mindedness as inter-related goals.

10 Dilemmas in Teaching with Discussion, pages 55–60
Copyright © 2016 by Information Age Publishing
All rights of reproduction in any form reserved.

Dilemma Map of Autonomy and Open-Mindedness in Discussion

In Figure 8.1, autonomy and open-mindedness within discussions are mapped. In the upper left quadrant, the positive benefits of autonomy are listed. In the upper right quadrant, the positive benefits of open-mindedness in discussions are given. In the lower left quadrant are the negative consequences of relying solely on autonomy as a goal is demonstrated, and in the lower right quadrant, the negative consequences of relying only on open-mindedness in discussions are provided.

Positive Quadrants

+ Upper Left	+ Upper Right
Perseverance Self-confidence Certainty and conviction Integrity Principled Self-determination and metacognition	Freshness/uniqueness Flexibility Compromise Humility Respect and tolerance Fairmindedness
Autonomy	**Open-mindedness**
Stubbornness Arrogance Beliefs Doctrine-focused	Vacillation of opinions with no convergence or sense of growth Ambivalence Doubt Unprincipled
– Lower Left	– Lower Right

Negative Quadrants

Figure 8.1 Dilemma map of autonomy and open-mindedness.

In the upper left quadrant of this dilemma map, the autonomy benefits of discussion are listed. A positive element of focusing upon intellectual autonomy (Paul, 1992; Paul & Elder, 2001) as an outcome of discussions is perseverance and self-confidence (Facione, 2000) in personal convictions. Discussion requires integrity, the realization of the need to be genuine to one's own thinking (Paul, 1993) once all aspects of an issue have been investigated. From in-depth exploration into others' perspectives and rational thinking, principled certainty and conviction develops. Additionally, self-determination and true metacognition regarding one's convictions is enhanced following a deep emergence into discussion.

In the upper right quadrant of this dilemma map, the benefits of open-mindedness in discussion are listed. John Dewey and colleagues (Dewey, 1916, p. 6) stated, "Try the experiment of communicating, with fullness and accuracy, some experience to another especially if it be somewhat complicated, and you will find your own attitude toward your experience changing." Good discussions encourage students to embody open-mindedness and a willingness to change their minds following deliberation (Leskes, 2013). There is an assumption of compromise with one who is open-minded. Moreover, open-mindedness supports fair-mindedness or the awareness of "the need to treat all viewpoints alike, without reference to one's own feelings or vested interests" (Paul, 1993, pp. 16–17). Open-mindedness promotes respect, tolerance, considerateness (Calhoun, 2000), and an intellectual flexibility that thrives on unique and novel ideas.

The lower left quadrant represents the negative outcomes of focusing solely on autonomy as a goal in discussion. Though instructors want their students to develop intellectual autonomy and integrity in their convictions from discussions, over-reliance on this side of the dilemma may result in stubbornness and arrogance regarding positions. Additionally, autonomy may only reflect beliefs, rather than measured reflection of knowledge and perspectives, if the other side of the dilemma is excluded from discussion. Rather than self-determination based on data and perspectives, students produce doctrinal dialogue grounded in little evidence.

The lower right quadrant represents the negative possibilities of valuing open-mindedness as an outcome of discussion. Instructors desire discussions that enhance students' willingness to hear and consider alternate paradigms and viewpoints. However, an over-use of this side of the dilemma may result in in wishy-washy and highly vacillated opinions that lack self-determinism and metacognition. When students only rely on open-mindedness in discussion, self-doubt, hesitancy in action, or immobilizing ambivalence may result. As a result, students may be viewed as unprincipled and non-action oriented.

There are clues that instructors and their students are spending too much time on one side or the other of the dilemma map. In the dilemma map, instructors who value only autonomy risk losing the benefits of open-mindedness—such as welcoming unique opinions. There are also clues that instructors and students have over-emphasized intellectual autonomy as an outcome. Students may display courage and conviction in discussions but lose flexibility, humility, and a disposition of freshness as they consider knowledge bound in reason and rationality. Clues that the instructor has over-relied on personal experiences are behaviors such as student comments that are self-referential only, and which lack the perspectives of outside research and theory. These clues are provided in Table 8.1 for autonomy and open-mindedness within discussion.

When instructors are unaware of dilemmas in instruction, they may focus on only one side of the map, unconsciously limiting the outcomes. In the dilemma map, teachers who value autonomy in discussions may be inflexible toward students who value open-mindedness and flexibility along with an orientation to engage with other perspectives that they do not share. Alternatively, instructors who value only open-mindedness miss important opportunities for students to develop intellectual courage and convictions, self-determination, and a commitment to principled actions and outcomes from discussion.

These clues help the instructor to move from the lower quadrants of this dilemma to the upper quadrants. For example, when the negative quadrant of autonomy as an outcome is being expressed too much, the instructor knows to move to open-mindedness as an instructional choice.

TABLE 8.1   Clues That Instructors Have Over-Relied on Either Autonomy or Open-Mindedness

Autonomy	Open-mindedness
1. Students make stubborn or arrogant statements. 2. Students ignore fair-mindedness by dialoguing without reference to the rational, critical, and diverse perspectives of others. 3. Expressions of are obviously based upon belief or doctrine, not consideration of facts, best practices, and perspectives.	1. Students sound overly hesitant or irresolute when expressing opinions after critical deliberation. 2. Students' expressions vacillate widely throughout the discussion and do not appear to converge at all. Students withdraw from discussion because of their ambivalence. 3. No convictions or action plans emerge from discussion. 4. Extreme cognitive dissonance results in immobility.

In the dilemma map, clues that the lower quadrant is being focused upon requires that the instructor move in a diagonal motion across to the upper quadrant where the positive outcomes of the dilemma may be addressed. Once behaviors are being expressed in the positive quadrant of the opposite side of the dilemma, move to the adjacent positive side to express both upper quadrants of the dilemma in the discussion, making the entire pedagogy more integral and complete. The map in Figure 8.2 demonstrates this conscious instructional choice from negative to positive quadrants.

Positive Quadrants

+ Upper Left	+ Upper Right
Perseverance	Freshness/uniqueness
Self-confidence	Flexibility
Certainty and conviction	Compromise
Integrity	Humility
Principled	Respect and tolerance
Self-determination and metacognition	Fairmindedness
Autonomy	**Open-mindedness**
Stubbornness	Vacillation of opinions with no convergence or sense of growth
Arrogance	Ambivalence
Beliefs	Doubt
Doctrine-focused	Unprincipled
− Lower Left	− Lower Right

Negative Quadrants

Figure 8.2 Moving to the positive quadrants.

Summary and Questions

Instructors may find value in both autonomy and open-mindedness as outcomes in discussion pedagogy. Both sides of the dilemma have positive outcomes, yet instructors must also be aware of and guard against the negative expressions of the instructional choice. Questions for instructors and their students within this dilemma are:

1. What are the benefits of students developing intellectual autonomy during discussion? What are the benefits of open-mindedness? Are there benefits to considering other points of view?
2. How can confidence in one's convictions improve discussion? How can open-mindedness be marginalized when autonomy alone is valued?
3. Why is flexibility and compromise valuable in discussions? How does humility protect against unexamined doctrine? Why does focusing solely on open-mindedness as an outcome threaten productive discussion?

9

Dialoguing and Questioning in Discussions

This chapter deals with the interconnected goals of dialoguing and questioning as reciprocal outcomes within discussion pedagogy. Varying forms of discussion instruction—from Freirean critical pedagogy, to Socratic legal education, to collaborative group processes—all value the interplay between dialoguing and questioning. Both dialoguing and questioning through collaborative endeavors are essential for integral discussion. Without students' willingness to speak their opinions and values, discussion becomes stymied, inauthentic, and pedagogically immature. Yet, instructors also want to create an instructional space where students use varying forms of questioning to investigate their own and other students' contentions. These goals are interdependent within discussions and must be reciprocally valued. A dilemma map demonstrates the positives and negatives of both sides of the dilemma. In addition, clues when an instructor is over-relying on one side of the map are provided, and a final visual demonstrates the movement from the lower quadrant to the appropriate upper quadrant when an instructor notices negative behaviors from the lower quadrants. The chapter ends with questions for discussion regarding dialoguing and questioning as mutual goals.

10 Dilemmas in Teaching with Discussion, pages 61–68
Copyright © 2016 by Information Age Publishing
All rights of reproduction in any form reserved.

Dilemma Map of Dialoguing and Questioning in Discussion

In Figure 9.1, dialoguing and questioning within discussions are mapped. In the upper left quadrant, the positive benefits of dialoguing are listed. In the upper right quadrant, the positive benefits of promoting questioning in discussions are given. In the lower left quadrant are the negative consequences of relying solely on dialogue as a goal, and in the lower right quadrant, the negative consequences of just questioning in discussions are provided.

In the upper left quadrant of this dilemma map, the benefits of dialoguing within discussion are listed. First, dialogue may lead to open and

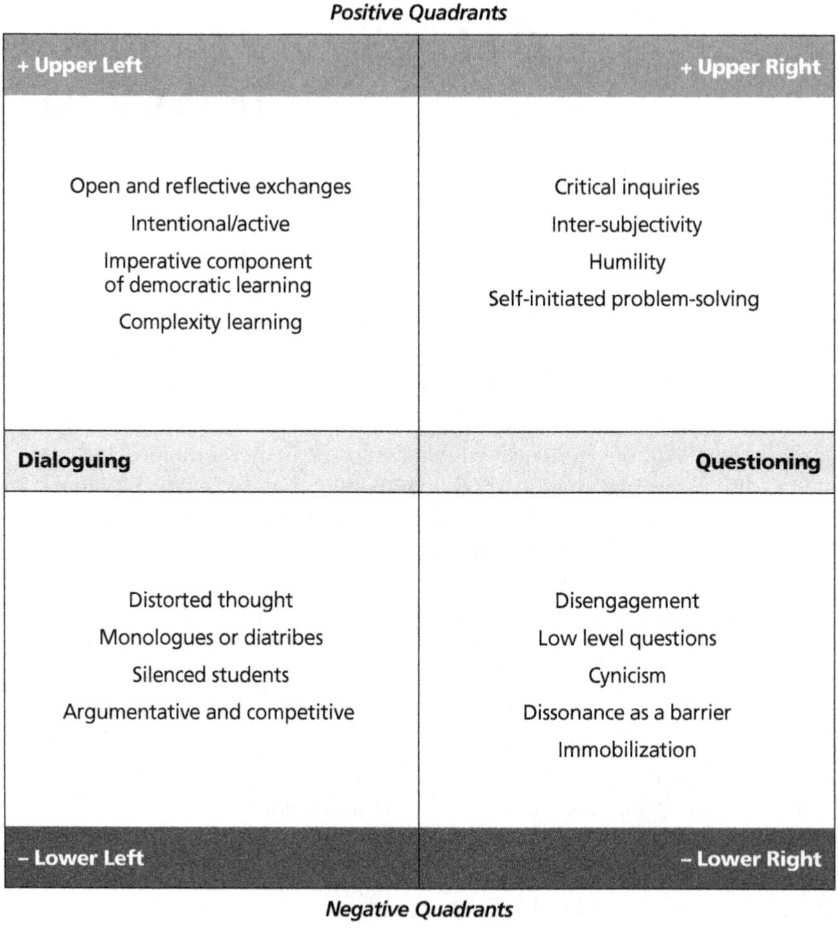

Positive Quadrants

+ Upper Left	+ Upper Right
Open and reflective exchanges Intentional/active Imperative component of democratic learning Complexity learning	Critical inquiries Inter-subjectivity Humility Self-initiated problem-solving
Dialoguing	**Questioning**
Distorted thought Monologues or diatribes Silenced students Argumentative and competitive	Disengagement Low level questions Cynicism Dissonance as a barrier Immobilization
– Lower Left	– Lower Right

Negative Quadrants

Figure 9.1 Dilemma map of dialoguing and questioning.

reflective exchanges of ideas which improve meaning making in learning. Just as deliberative democracies require dialogue to make manifest varying political and social realities, discussion requires students to deliberatively dialogue about their own assumptions and values. Dialogue permits a way of settling differences, promoting empathy and understanding for others, comparing alternative hypotheses, collaborating about differences, and engaging with oneself and with other perspectives (Burbules, 2000). Dialogue is intentional and active when used in pedagogy. It supports the notion of participation in a democratic learning space where one has the responsibility to put forth one's contentions as part of a larger goal toward civil discourse on difficult and controversial issues. In dialogue that encourages this deliberation, it is a key factor for creating democratic learning spaces that embrace diversity and inspires perspective building. It encourages both autonomy of thought and open-mindedness. Last, the interactions between speaker and listener shape future dialogue and actions, resulting in a paradigm of complexity as an anticipated outcome of discussion. The interactive nature of speaking and listening in dialogue suggests that this form of instruction is bound in a systems-theory orientation as speakers and other students observe their own interactional social system of communication (Luhmann, 2008). Through dialogue, students acknowledge their own place within the class as interdependent and variable components (Ng, 2014) of a larger complex system, both as a class and as members of the larger community and culture.

A focus on the upper right quadrant of the dilemma map reveals the positive outcomes of balancing questioning as an outcome and process of discussion. Questioning can be found in many pedagogical traditions. Socrates used questions to demand that students analyze their own beliefs to engender true knowledge rather than simple personal convictions (Plato, 1937). Socratic questioning as a component of Socratic dialogue has been recognized as a method for developing critical analysis (Golding, 2011; Knezic, Wubbels, Elbers, & Hajer, 2010; Paul & Elder, 2007). A hierarchical taxonomic approach to questioning (Bloom et al., 1956) is widely used in educational circles to encourage the higher order thinking skills of synthesis and evaluation. More recently, essential questions to guide lessons have become common (McTighe & Wiggins, 2013). Questioning gives reliability to the idea that contextual knowing is a process of inquiring and establishing the reasonableness of a belief (Burbles, 1991).

The benefits of questioning within discussions are numerous. First, questioning allows students to evaluate their own opinions, as well as those of other students, with critical analysis. Critical thinking may be defined in many ways, but researchers seem to concur that using questions to scrutinize formal reasoning is a central defining attribute (Lai, 2011; Paul, Binker, Martin, & Adamson, 1989). Universal Intellectual Standards (Elder & Paul, 2007) help check the quality of reasoning in discussion and include: clarity, accuracy, precision, relevance, depth, breadth, logic, significance, and fairness of expression. Probing questions accompany each standard such as "Could you elaborate further? (Clarity)"; "How does that relate to the problem? (Relevance)"; and "Is this the central idea to focus on? (Significance)" (p. 5). Each level of the Universal Intellectual Standards may be systematically addressed by students and the instructor to explore the assertions that are expressed (Anderson & Piro, 2014; Piro & Anderson, 2015).

Second, when instructors ask students to incorporate varying levels of follow-up questions to student pronouncements in dialogue, they encourage inter-subjectivity by considering others' perspectives and values. Questioning interrupts the purely subjective nature of dialogue and rearranges the orientation from the self to others. With this inter-subjective orientation, intellectual humility is fostered, which is the knowledge of one's own limitations in knowledge and the tendency to self-deceive when only an egotistic viewpoint is expressed through dialogue (Paul, 1993). Last, questioning encourages self-initiated problem solving as it assists students to discover the answers they already possess (Navia, 1985) and to question the contentions of others, leading to self-directed problem solving.

The lower left quadrant represents the negative outcomes of focusing solely on dialoguing in discussion. Collaborative student learning is supported by social constructivists who maintain that learning does not occur in isolation (Vygotsky, 2006). Yet, students often use fallacious logic within their dialogue, and discussions can devolve into repositories of distorted thought (Piro & Anderson, 2015). Instead of increasing true dialogue, discussions that focus exclusively on individual student talk may result in monologues or diatribes that increase polarization rather than fostering compromise and empathy (Hibbing & Theiss-Morse, 2002). Additionally, dialogue may be limited as a means of exchange for some students, specifically for women, nonwhite students, and those who do not engage in dialogue. For varying reasons, these students are excluded and disadvantaged by classroom discussions (Burbules, 2000). Rather than dialogue being an individual "choice" in class, dialoguing may be more about systemic preferences for speaking that emerge from the larger cultural context where some students feel more privileged to speak than others. For example, it has been suggested that women prefer a more non-confrontational process than the competitive and adversarial approach to the verbal disagreements within discussion (see, for example, Belenky, 1986; Ellsworth, 1989; Gore, 1993; Gilligan, 1982; Noddings, 1984; Tannen & Leapman, 1998). Dialogue, with its innate active and controversial processes, may result more in silence than active engagement. Students who feel hesitant to express their views that are based in marginalized, rather than dominant, discourses may choose to remain silent rather than engage, creating a political silence that springs from deep dissent (Lewis, 1993) when students are dissatisfied with dominant expressions in discussion.

The lower right quadrant represents the negative possibilities of valuing only questioning as an outcome of discussion. When instructors and students pose challenging questions, students may not understand the content or form of the question, and may interpret the questions as threatening and potentially stressful. Some students may be unwilling to submit to the questioning of their perspectives in a public forum such as discussion and may interpret the questions as personal attacks. Additionally, the level of complexity of questions is central to good discussion. When low-level or inappropriate questions are thrown into the exchanges, the discussion quality suffers and may result in inauthentic and forced interchanges. Another negative outcome is that a focus only on questioning may lead to an attitude of cynicism that makes arriving at a conclusion about one's thoughts challenging. Questioning one's long-held assumptions and questioning other's beliefs does not automatically result in a convergent attitude or conviction regarding the issue. Cognitive dissonance is a necessary experience of discussion pedagogy and heralds growth and the development of complexity of thought. However, too much cognitive dissonance can interrupt learning and result in the restriction of thought processes. Non-action or non-application to one's own contexts and circumstances following the discussion may result, with the only true outcome being sarcasm, skepticism, and/or immobilization.

There are clues that instructors and their students are spending too much time on one side or the other of the dilemma map. In the dilemma map, instructors who value only dialoguing lose the benefits of critical questioning. Participants may speak in discussions that promote student voice. However, this dialogue may be distorted, irrational, or perpetuate existing stereotypes. There are also clues that instructors and students have overrelied on questioning. Students may become cynical and disengaged, and may express confusion with the issues being discussed. These clues are provided in Table 9.1 for dialogue and questioning within discussion.

When instructors are unaware of dilemmas in instruction, they may focus on only one side of the map, unconsciously limiting the goals and outcomes. In the dilemma map, teachers who value dialogue in discussions may be inflexible toward students who do not engage in the discussion, or who do not appear active in their own meaning making through dialogue,

TABLE 9.1   Clues That Instructors Have Over-Relied on Either Dialogue or Questioning

Dialoguing	Questioning
1. Student dialogue is unreflexive and/or irrational. 2. Students produce monologues. 3. Students voice diatribes against various points of view or those they consider to be out-groups. 4. Existing stereotypes and prejudices are perpetuated. 5. Student dialogue seems stymied in that various positions are voiced, but no one seems influenced by the expressions of others. 6. The dialogue seems to be confrontational or overly argumentative. 7. The discussion appears more like a debate than a discussion. 8. Various students do not engage in the dialogue at all.	1. Constant questioning of perspectives negatively affects the engagement of students. 2. Students appear confused by the questions. 3. Students interpret the questions as personal attacks rather than questions about stances. 4. Low-level or inappropriate questions do not further the discussion or enhance the development of complex and nuanced viewpoints. 5. Students appear caught in a continual loop and are unable to come to a judgement or to engage in action from the discussion.

or those who embrace their own intellectual humility. Alternatively, instructors who over-value questioning as a goal of discussion may marginalize the significance of actually having the courage and autonomy to state one's own thoughts about assumptions and values. Instructors who only value questioning risk losing these instructional dynamics that can create an active student voice and intentional articulation of one's perspective, the cornerstone of discussion.

These clues help the instructor to move from the lower quadrants of this dilemma to the upper quadrant. For example, when the negative quadrant of dialoguing as an outcome is being expressed too much, the instructor knows to move to focusing on questioning in instructional choices. In the dilemma map, clues that the negative expressions of the lower quadrant are being expressed require that the instructor move in a diagonal motion across to the upper quadrant where the positive outcomes of the dilemma may be addressed. Once behaviors are regularly evident in the positive quadrant of the opposite side of the dilemma, move to the adjacent positive side to express both upper quadrants of the dilemma in the discussion, making the entire pedagogy more integral and complete. The map in Figure 9.2 demonstrates this conscious instructional choice from negative to positive quadrants.

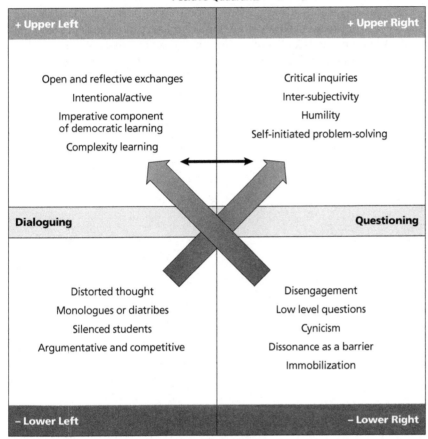

Figure 9.2   Moving to the positive quadrants.

Summary and Questions

Instructors may find value in both dialoguing and questioning in discussion pedagogy. Both sides of the dilemma have positive outcomes, yet instructors must also be aware of and guard against the negative expressions of the instructional choice. Questions for instructors and their students within this dilemma are:

1. What are the benefits of students being encouraged to actively dialogue in discussion? What are the benefits asking students to question their own and other's contentions?

2. How can dialogue be viewed as intentional and active in nature? Why is the ability to voice one's opinions important for democratic learning spaces? How can dialogue embrace complexity learning?
3. What are the benefits of scaffolding critical analysis of one's and other's contentions through varying levels of questions? Why does questioning encourage self-initiated problem solving?

10

Whole and Small Groups in Discussions

This chapter deals with the interconnected goals of both whole group and small group discussion pedagogy. Whole group refers to discussion with the entire class. Small group discussion refers to any grouping of students from dyads, to small groupings, to fishbowl arrangements. These goals are interdependent within discussions and must be reciprocally valued; moving between both types of discussions enhances the other. A dilemma map demonstrates the positives and negatives of both sides of the dilemma. In addition, clues when an instructor is over-relying on one side of the map are provided, and a final visual demonstrates the movement from the lower quadrant to the appropriate upper quadrant when an instructor notices negative behaviors from the lower quadrants. The chapter ends with questions for discussion regarding whole and small groups in discussion.

10 Dilemmas in Teaching with Discussion, pages 69–74
Copyright © 2016 by Information Age Publishing
All rights of reproduction in any form reserved.

Dilemma Map of Whole and Small Group Discussion

In Figure 10.1, whole and small groups within discussions are mapped. In the upper left quadrant, the positive benefits of whole groups as an instructional arrangement are listed. In the upper right quadrant, the positive benefits of small group discussions are given. In the lower left quadrant are the negative consequences of relying solely on whole groups and, in the lower right quadrant, the negative consequences of relying only on small groups in discussions are provided.

In the upper left quadrant of this dilemma map, the product benefits of using whole group discussions are listed. In a whole classroom discussion,

Positive Quadrants

+ Upper Left	+ Upper Right
Unified schema/curriculum Common directions Broader and alternative perspectives Time efficient Instructor–student dialogue	Rehearsal Student interactions Local/"parts" focus of curriculum Divergent directions Focused perspectives Student–student dialogue
Whole Group	**Small Group**
Dominant speakers Dominant paradigms Too much teacher–student talk	No common curriculum Narrowed focus Time luxury Too much student–student talk
– Lower Left	– Lower Right

Negative Quadrants

Figure 10.1   Dilemma map of whole and small group learning.

the instructor can begin with a common concept for discussion and a joint instructional focus, such as using an advanced organizer. This shared instructional activity may subsequently foster divergent connections as each student brings his or her own schema to the learning (Ausubel, Novak, & Hanesian, 1968). Additionally, this whole class setting promotes common curricular and assessment outcomes with potentially broader, richer, more complex, and more diverse points of view. Last, a whole class focus for discussion may be time efficient by allowing the instructor the autonomy to cover required content and quickly manage dialogue that is off focus through effective teacher–student speech.

In the upper right quadrant of this dilemma map, the benefits of small group dynamics in discussion are listed. Small group discussion can take many forms: dyads, silent reflection then pair-shares, three to five person buzz groups, syndicates, even Socratic circles with a smaller group discussion in a fishbowl where students on the outside replace students on the inside of the circle. Each small group arrangement has advantages for discussion. One of the benefits of each format is that students have the ability to rehearse individual parts of learning from the whole group discussion, promoting long-term memory storage through personal engagement (Gage & Berliner, 1984). Small groups also support individual student or localized perspectives that may not emerge in large group discussions because the small group enhances safety and a sense of belonging. This development of diverse perspectives within smaller discussion groupings may additionally encourage a more enhanced and engaged focus on topics that is supported by student–student dialogue.

The lower left quadrant represents the negative outcomes of focusing solely on whole class discussions. There is the potential for speakers to dominate the whole group discussion, allowing fewer entries into dialogue and narrowing the perspectives of the discussion to those the dominant speakers choose. The paradigms that are marginalized in society may never emerge if dominant speakers do not raise them, and the entire discussion is centered in their taken-for-granted assumptions regarding cultural, gendered, racial, and ethnic experiences. Power inequities that are institutionalized in society seep into whole class discussions. Last, too much instructor-teacher speech and facilitation is a potential pitfall of whole group discussions in that it does not center on self-regulation and growth.

The lower right quadrant represents the negative possibilities of valuing only small group dynamics in discussion. Small group dynamics promote individual participation and engagement. However, students may not cover necessary content; they may focus on their own personal perspectives without hearing broader ones; and because small group dynamics require time, some instructors find this discussion arrangement to be a luxury they cannot afford. This lower quadrant of the dilemma map suggests that sometimes student–student talk may be unproductive.

There are clues that instructors and their students are spending too much time on one side or the other of the dilemma map. In the dilemma map, instructors who value only whole group discussion risk losing the benefits of the small group—local knowledge and a more focused, and perhaps more in-depth, understanding of some topics. Instructors who over emphasize small group discussions as an instructional arrangement of the discussion lose valuable outcomes in whole discussion instruction. For example, students may not convene back into the whole discussion with common understandings or sufficient curriculum coverage due to the local emphasis and time usage for small group discussions.

The clues that instructors have over-relied on one side of the dilemma map are provided in Table 10.1.

When instructors are unaware of dilemmas in instruction, they may focus on only one side of the map, unconsciously limiting the outcomes. In the dilemma map, teachers who value whole group discussions may be inflexible toward students who prefer expression in small groups, thus marginalizing the significance of their specific perspectives and experiences. Alternatively, instructors who only value small group discussions miss important opportunities for students to engage with common experiences of the curriculum and content with instructor guidance.

These clues help the instructor to move from the lower quadrants of this dilemma to the upper quadrant. For example, when the negative

TABLE 10.1 Clues That Instructors Have Over-Relied on Either Whole Group or Small Group Discussion

Whole Group	Small Group
1. One or a few speakers dominate the whole group discussion. 2. Students' dialogue is grounded only in dominant paradigms. Students do not put forth experiences or research that is unexamined or marginalized by society. 3. Some students appear unengaged or bored. 4. Instructors dominate the flow of dialogue and insufficient student talk occurs, or talk is simply oriented toward instructor interests.	1. Students are unable to make connections to the larger curriculum goals. 2. Students' expressions are comprehensible only to themselves, and not to the larger whole group. 3. Too much student–student talk occurs without the guidance of the instructor.

quadrant of whole group discussion is being expressed too much, the instructor knows to move to small group instructional choices. In the dilemma map, clues that the lower quadrant is being focused upon requires that the instructor move in a diagonal motion across to the upper quadrant where the positive outcomes of the dilemma may be addressed. Once behaviors are being expressed in the positive quadrant of the opposite side of the dilemma, move to the adjacent positive side to express both upper quadrants of the dilemma in the discussion, making the entire pedagogy more integral and complete. The map in Figure 10.2 demonstrates this conscious instructional choice from negative to positive quadrants.

Positive Quadrants

+ Upper Left	+ Upper Right
Unified schema/curriculum	Rehearsal
Common directions	Student interactions
Broader and alternative perspectives	Local/"parts" focus of curriculum
Time efficient	Divergent directions
Instructor–student dialogue	Focused perspectives
	Student–student dialogue
Whole Group	**Small Group**
Dominant speakers	No common curriculum
Dominant paradigms	Narrowed focus
Too much teacher–student talk	Time luxury
	Too much student–student talk
– Lower Left	– Lower Right

Negative Quadrants

Figure 10.2 Moving to the positive quadrants.

Summary and Questions

Instructors may find value in both whole group and small group discussion pedagogy. Both sides of the dilemma have positive outcomes, yet instructors must also be aware of, and guard against, the negative expressions of the instructional choice. Questions for instructors and their students within this dilemma are:

1. What are the benefits of students interacting with common concepts and organizers in whole group discussion? What are the benefits of teacher–student talk?
2. Why is small group discussion a benefit for many students? What is the value of student–student talk?

CONCLUSION

Recommendations for Managing Integral Instruction

We will not be able to teach in the power of paradox until we are willing
to suffer the tension of opposites, until we understand that such suffering is neither
to be avoided nor merely to be survived but must be actively embraced
for the way it expands our own hearts.
—Parker Palmer, (1998)

A paradox has "contradictory, yet integrated elements that exist simultaneously and persist over time" (Smith & Lewis, 2011, pg. 382). As Parker Palmer suggested above, a paradox needs to be embraced, not avoided. Paradoxes are simultaneously interdependent and separate. They require a complexity of thought and action that cherishes tensions and integration. Embracing contradictions for a more integral pedagogy is a natural outcome of discussion pedagogy that values paradox and dilemma.

The dilemma maps in the previous chapters demonstrate that the contradictions of instructional choices and student outcomes are mutually

10 Dilemmas in Teaching with Discussion, pages 75–78
Copyright © 2016 by Information Age Publishing
All rights of reproduction in any form reserved.

interactive and achievable in discussion pedagogy. The paradox is that instructors do not need to choose either one side of the dilemma OR the other. The goal of polarity mapping, according to Johnson (1998), is to attempt to recognize the benefits of both polarities and to purposefully and intentionally remain in the upper quadrants, thereby maximizing the benefits of each polarity. I modified Johnson's polarity map for organizational issues with a dilemma map, a map that demonstrates instructional choices for ten instructional dilemmas in discussion. Additionally, by recognizing the negative outcomes of each polarity, as displayed in the bottom quadrants, one can intentionally avoid the consequences of over-relying on those sides of the map. The shift to both/and thinking—focusing on both sides of the dilemmas and also on the positive and negative outcomes for each polarity within the polarity mapping quadrants—allows instructors to negotiate the interdependent poles of using discussion instruction within their classrooms.

Teaching with discussion pedagogy is a complex instructional strategy. Instructional choices—such as teaching with a structured or unstructured formats—and instructional goals— such as focusing on individual and relational learning or only dialoguing or questioning—are part of the ongoing management processes that further complicate the pedagogy. I offer some recommendations for using dilemma management in discussion pedagogy.

First, reflect upon your own use of discussion. Consider which of the key dilemmas in discussion pedagogy are more commonly used in your instruction. Perhaps students have been focused on engaging in dialogue and expressing opinions but have not consistently used self or peer questioning to further the dialogue. Or perhaps students have been true to their own expressions by demonstrating intellectual autonomy, but have not consistently practiced open-mindedness by treating other opinions with a receptive attitude. Noticing where the instructor or students are addressing one dilemma over the other is the place to start.

Second, after choosing a dilemma to focus upon, refer to the dilemma map for that key discussion dilemma. Recognize the positive outcomes for both sides of the dilemma, then consider the negative outcomes. From this map, create instructional choices that highlight both the upper quadrants of the map. For example, if discussions have typically been structured, purposefully allow an organic discussion with fewer time or content restrictions. Discover the unanticipated outcomes of an unstructured discussion, while mindfully being aware of the negative quadrant outcomes for unstructured discussions as well.

Next, recognize that using dilemma mapping in instruction is process-oriented as well as product-oriented. Allow both instructor and student dissonances as competing dilemmas are investigated, being mindful of when that disruption becomes unproductive rather than helpful. Although cognitive dissonance is a driver of dilemma management, ambiguity can trigger discomfort. Working with incompatible ideas and notions outside of one's current capacity engages both the cognitive and emotional processes, but the uncertainty necessary to consider competing discourses within discussion may be distressing for some students. Practice patience for yourself and for your students while expanding your repertoire of instruction through dilemma management of discussions.

Fourth, explicitly teach the dilemmas of discussion to students. Engaging students in instructional choices may encourage the positive outcomes and goals of dilemma mapping. Students may provide formal or informal feedback to the instructor when it is appropriate to switch poles in the dilemma. Using the focused questions to explore each dilemma with your students inspires a meta-discussion about discussion as an instructional practice.

Last, actively embrace the complexities of discussion instruction. Dilemma mapping may be viewed as a component of complexity theory (Dent, 1999; Ng, 2014), which suggests that learning is complex and consists of interdependent parts that should not be reduced to individual components. Viewing the dilemmas as interconnected parts of a whole pedagogy provides a more balanced outcome. As Senge, a systems-thinker, commented: "[T]he unhealthiness of our world today is in direct proportion to our inability to see it as a whole" (Senge, 1990, p. 68). Teaching students about complex and integral choices in discussion will likely increase meta cognition and meta engagement; in fact, meta discussions about each of the polarities of discussion are realistic complexity-based and holistic outcomes.

Discussion pedagogy involves an exchange of ideas about conflicting views, beliefs, and values among students (Hess & McAvoy, 2014; McAvoy & Hess, 2013; Watt, 2007). While discussion instruction is complex, it also affords opportunities for reflection and growth about the dilemmas inherent in the instructional processes and the student outcomes of discussion, rather than viewing the contradictions as problems to get through. Integrative thinking is largely a tacit skill occurring in the heads of people who consciously cultivate management of polarities (Martin, 2009) and, as such, discussion instruction fosters integrative results. Dilemma management focuses on sustaining contradictions rather than avoiding ambiguity by valuing the paradoxes and welcoming the dilemmas, rather than ignoring or downplaying them. It embraces mindsets oriented toward integral rather than simple oppositional thought. Dilemma mapping in discussion instruction helps students to negotiate the spaces between pedagogical choices that appear conflicting, but which are interdependent and promote wholeness in outcomes.

By unequivocally modeling polarity management in discussion instruction, the instructor promotes the students' abilities to simultaneously hold opposing viewpoints in perspective while they continue their investigation of topics, demonstrating inquisitiveness and open-mindedness *and* courage and self-determination as part of the integrative outcomes of discussion. When instructors model the processes of managing dilemmas, they accomplish exactly what functioning discussions should achieve. They demonstrate that people from opposing camps can discuss, leading to more holistic mindsets and more complex actions as outcomes.

Discussions can be inter-subjective, multi-perspectival, and complex pedagogy when dilemma management is intentionally and systematically incorporated into the planning of instructional processes and the consideration of student outcomes. Discussions work best when an instructor incorporates both sides of the dilemma, resulting in a dialectical pedagogy that is complex and holistic. Within a dilemma management framework of discussion instruction, students have the opportunity to explore their own values, assumptions, and processes as well as contribute within democratic spaces. They are able to manage difference in a new way. With this opportunity, discussion pedagogy enhances integral and holistic mindsets for students.

References

Adler, M. J. (1998). *Paideia proposal.* New York, NY: Simon and Schuster.

Anderson, G., & Piro, J. (2014). *Jigsaw Socrates café for diversity and social justice. Encyclopedia of Diversity and Social Justice Project.* Lanham, MD: Rowman & Littlefield.

Anderson, G., & Piro, J. S. (in press). A case study investigating the demands and challenges of critical thinking instruction. In L. Trujillo-Jenks & R. Fredrickson (Eds.) *Case Studies: Working through Current School Issues.*

Anderson, G., & Piro, J. S. (2015). A partnership in a pedagogy of process: Conversations about co-teaching critical analysis. *Journal of Interdisciplinary Education, 14*(1), 72–94.

Ausubel, D. P., Novak, J. D., & Hanesian, H. (1968). *Educational psychology: A cognitive view.* New York, NY: Holt, Reinhart, & Wintston.

Belenky, M. F. (1986). *Women's ways of knowing: The development of self, voice, and mind.* New York, NY: Basic Books.

Bloom, B. S., Engelhart, M. D., Furst, E. J., Hill, W. H., & Krathwohl, D. R. (1956). *Taxonomy of educational objectives: Handbook I: Cognitive domain.* New York, NY: David McKay.

Brookfield, S. D., & Preskill, S. (2012). *Discussion as a way of teaching: Tools and techniques for democratic classrooms.* Hoboken, NJ: John Wiley & Sons.

Burbules, N. (1991) Rationality and reasonableness: A discussion of Harvey Siegel's relativism refuted and educating reason. *Educational Theory, 41*(2), 235–252.

10 Dilemmas in Teaching with Discussion, pages 79–84

Copyright © 2016 by Information Age Publishing
All rights of reproduction in any form reserved.

Burbules, N. C. (2000). The limits of dialogue as a critical pedagogy. In P. Trifonas (Ed.), *Revolutionary pedagogies: Cultural politics, education, and the discourse of theory*, New York, NY: Psychology Press.

Calhoun, C. (2000). The virtue of civility. *Philosophy & Public Affairs, 29*(3), 251–275.

Capra, F. (2003). *The hidden connections*. London, UK: Flamingo.

Crowl, T. K., Kaminsky, S., & Podell, D. M. (1997). *Educational psychology: Windows on teaching*. Madison, WI: Brown and Benchmark.

Dahlberg, L. (2001). The Internet and democratic discourse: Exploring the prospects of online deliberative forums extending the public sphere. *Information, Communication & Society, 4*(4), 615–633.

Darling-Hammond, L. (1996). The right to learn and the advancement of teaching: Research, policy, and practice for democratic education. *Educational Researcher, 6*(25), 5–17. http://dx.doi.org/10.3102/001318 9X025006005

Dewey, J. (1916). *Democracy in educatin*. New York, NY: McMillian Press.

Dewey, J. (1933). *How we think*. Buffalo, NY: Prometheus Books. (Original work published 1910)

Dewey, J. (1944). *Democracy and education*. New York, NY: Free Press. (Original work published 1910)

Dewey, J., Boydston, J., Baysinger, P., Levine, B., & Hook, S. (2008). *The middle works, 1899–1924*. Carbondale, IL: Southern Illinois University Press.

Dent, E. B. (1999). Complexity science: A worldview shift. *Emergence, 1*(4), 5–19.

Doll, W. E. (1993). *A post-modern perspective on curriculum* (Vol. 167). New York, NY: Teachers College Press.

Dryek, J. (1996). *Democracy in capitalist times: Ideals, limits, and struggles*. New York, NY: Oxford University Press.

Dunn, R., Dunn, K., & Price, G. E. (1977). *Diagnosing learning styles: A prescription for avoiding malpractice suits*. Bloomington, IN: Phi Delta Kappan.

Elder, L., & Paul, R. (2007). Universal intellectual standards. *The critical thinking community*. Retrieved from http://www. criticalthinking. org/articles/ universalintellectual-standards.cfm

Elder, L. & Paul, R. (2008). *Intellectual standards: The words that name them and the criteria that define them*. Dillon Beach, CA: Foundation for Critical Thinking.

Ellsworth, E. (1989). Why doesn't this feel empowering? Working through the repressive myths of critical pedagogy. *Harvard Educational Review, 59*(3), 297–325.

Facione, P. A. (1990). *Critical thinking: A statement of expert consensus for purposes of educational assessment and instruction*. Millbrae, CA: California Academic Press.

Facione, P. A. (2000). The disposition toward critical thinking: Its character, measurement, and relationship to critical thinking skill. *Informal Logic, 20*(1), 61–84.

Farrell, J. T. (1959). *Dialogue on John Dewey*. C. Lamont (Ed.). New York, NY: Horizon Press.

Fitzgerald, F. S. (2009). *The crack-up*. New York, NY: New Directions Publishing. Retrieved from http://isites.harvard.edu/fs/docs/icb.topic1069083.files/Unit%20II%20Readings/The%20Crack-Up.pdf

Foucault, M. (1980). Truth and power. In C. Gordon, (Ed.) *Power/knowledge: Selected interviews* (pp. 63–77). New York, NY: Pantheon Books.

Freeman, P. D. (2004). *Wrestling with both/and: A case study on the impacts of polarity thinking for a corporate leadership team* (Unpublished doctoral dissertation). University of St. Thomas, St. Paul, MN.

Freire, P. (1993). *Pedagogy of the oppressed*. New York, NY: Continuum. (Original work published 1970)

Gage, N. L., & Berliner, D. C. (1984). *Educational psychology* (3rd ed.). New York, NY: Houghton Mifflin.

Gilligan, C. (1982). *In a different voice: Psychological theory and women's development*. Cambridge, MA: Harvard University Press.

Golding, C. (2011). Educating for critical thinking: Thought-encouraging questions in a community of inquiry. *Higher Education Research & Development, 30*(3), 357–370.

Goleman, D. (2006). *Emotional intelligence*. New York, NY: Bantam Books.

Gore, J. (1993). *The struggle for pedagogies: Critical and feminist discourses as regimes of truth*. New York, NY: Routledge.

Hess, D. E. (2009). *Controversy in the classroom: The democratic power of discussion*. New York, NY: Routledge.

Hess, D. E., & McAvoy, P. (2014). Should teachers help students develop partisan identities? *Social Education, 78*(6), 293–297.

Hibbing, J. R., & Theiss-Morse, E. (2002). *Stealth democracy: Americans' beliefs about how government should work*. Cambridge, UK: Cambridge University Press.

hooks, b. (1989). *Talking back: Thinking feminist, thinking black*. Brooklyn, NY: South End Press.

Jacobs, J. E., & Paris, S. G. (1987). Children's metacognition about reading: Issues in definition, measurement, and instruction. *Educational Psychologist, 22*(3–4), 255–278.

Janis, I. (1972). *Victims of groupthink: A psychological study of foreign-policy decisions and fiascoes*. Oxford, UK: Houghton Mifflin.

Johnson, B. (1992). *Polarity management: Identifying and managing unsolvable problems*. Amherst, MA: Human Resource Development Press.

Johnson, B. (1998). *Polarity management: A summary introduction*. Middleville, MI: Polarity Management Associates.

Joseph, D. L., & Newman, D. A. (2010). Emotional intelligence: An integrative meta-analysis and cascading model. *Journal of Applied Psychology, 95*(1), 54.

Jung, C. G. (1986). On the nature of the psyche. In H. Read, M. Fordham, & G. Adler (Eds.), *C. G. Jung: The collected works* (Vol. 8, pp. 159–234) (R. F. C. Hull, Trans., 2nd ed.). London, UK: Routledge and Kegan Paul.

Kelly, U. (1997). *Schooling desire.* New York, NY: Routledge.

Kilduff, M., Chiaburu, D. S., & Menges, J. I. (2010). Strategic use of emotional intelligence in organizational settings: Exploring the dark side. *Research in Organizational Behavior, 30,* 129–152.

Knezic, D., Wubbels, T., Elbers, E., & Hajer, M. (2010). The Socratic dialogue and teacher education. *Teaching and Teacher Education, 26*(4), 1104–1111.

Koestler, A. (1967). *The ghost in the machine.* London, UK: Hutchinson.

Laiken, M. E. (2002). *Managing the action/reflection polarity through dialogue: A path to transformative learning* (NALL Working Paper #53-2002). Research Network on New Approaches to Lifelong Learning, Ontario Institute for Studies in Education of the University of Toronto. Retrieved from http://nall.oise.utoronto.ca/res/53MarilynLaiken.pdf.

Lai, E. (2011). Critical thinking: A literature review. *Pearson's Research Reports,* 6.

Lao Tsu. (1972). *Lao Tsu-Tao Te Ching.* G. F. Feng & J. English (Trans.). New York, NY: Knopf.

Lawrence, P. R., & Lorsch, J. W. (1967). Differentiation and integration in complex organizations. *Administrative Science Quarterly, 12*(1), 1–47. Retrieved from http://dx.doi.org/10.2307/2391211

Leskes, A. (2013). A plea for civil discourse: Needed, the academy's leadership. *LiberalEducation, 99*(4). Retrieved from http://www.aacu.org/liberaleducation/le-fa13/leskes.cfm

Lewis, M. (1993). *Without a word: Teaching beyond women's silence.* New York, NY: Routledge.

Luhmann, N. (2008). The autopoiesis of social systems. *Journal of Sociocybernetics, 6*(2), 84–95.

LeDoux, J. (1998). *The emotional brain: The mysterious underpinnings of emotional life.* New York, NY: Simon and Schuster.

McAvoy, P., & Hess, D. E. (2013). Classroom deliberation in an era of political polarization. *Curriculum Inquiry, 43*(1), 14–47. Retrieved from http://dx.doi.org/10.1111/curi.2013.43.issue-1

McGregor, D. M. (1957). The human side of enterprise. *The Management Review, 46*(11), 22–28.

McTighe, J., & Wiggins, G. (2013). *Essential questions: Opening doors to student understanding.* Alexandria, VA: Association for Supervision and Curriculum Development.

Martin, R. L. (2009). *The opposable mind: Winning through integrative thinking.* Boston, MA: Harvard Business Press.

Marzano, R. J., Brandt, R. S., Hughes, C. S., Jones, B. F., Presseisen, C. S., Rankin, S. C., & Suhor, C. (1988). *Dimensions of thinking: A framework for curriculum and instruction.* Alexandria, VA: Association for Supervision and Curriculum Development.

Meier, D. (2002). *The power of their ideas: Lessons for America from a small school in Harlem.* Boston, MA: Beacon Press.

Menges, J. I., Kilduff, M., Kern, S., & Bruch, H. (2015). The awestruck effect: Followers suppress emotion expression in response to charismatic but not individually considerate leadership. *The Leadership Quarterly, 26*(4), 626–640.

Navia, L. E. (1985). *Socrates: The man and his philosophy.* Lanham, MD: The University Press of America.

Nikitina, L. (2012). Addressing pedagogical dilemmas in a constructivist language learning experience. *Journal of the Scholarship of Teaching and Learning, 10*(2), 90–106.

Noddings, N. (1984). *Caring: A feminine approach to ethics and moral education.* Berkeley and Los Angeles, CA: University of California Press.

Ng, F. S. D. (2014). Complexity-based learning—An alternative learning design for the twenty-first century. *Cogent Education, 1*(1). DOI: 10.1080/2331186X.2014.970325

Palmer, P. (1998). *The courage to teach.* San Francisco, CA: Josey Bass.

Parker, W. C., & Hess, D. (2001). Teaching with and for discussion. *Teaching and Teacher Education, 17*(3), 273–289.

Parker, W. C. (2005). Teaching against idiocy. *Phi Delta Kappan, 86*(5), 344–351.

Pascale, R. T. (1990). *Managing on the edge.* New York, NY: Simon and Schuster.

Paul, R. (1992), Critical thinking: What, why, and how. *New Directions for Community Colleges, 77,* 3–24. doi: 10.1002/cc.3681992770

Paul, R. (1993). *Critical thinking.* Santa Rosa, CA: Foundation for Critical Thinking.

Paul, R., Binker, A. J. A., Martin, D., & Adamson, K. (1989). *Critical thinking handbook: Higher school, a guide for redesigning instruction.* Rohnert Park, CA: Center for Critical Thinking and Moral Critique, Sonoma State University.

Paul, R., & Elder, L. (2001). *The miniature guide to critical thinking: Concepts & tools* (Vol. 2). Tomales, CA: Foundation for Critical Thinking.

Paul, R., & Elder, L. (2007). Critical thinking: The art of Socratic questioning. *Journal of Developmental Education, 31*(1), 34–37.

Phillips, C. (2001). *Socrates café: A fresh taste of philosophy.* New York, NY: Norton.

Plato. (1937). The apology. (B. Jowett, Trans.) In C. W. Eliot (Ed.), *The Harvard Classics.* New York, NY: Collier & Son.

Piro, J. S., & Anderson, G. (2015). Discussions in Socrates café: Implications for critical thinking in teacher education. *Action in Teacher Education. 37*(3), 265–283.

Piro, J. S., & Anderson, G. (in press). A typology for an online Socrates Café. *Teachers College Record 118*(7).

Roberts, T., & Billings, L. (1999). *The Paideia classroom: Teaching for understanding.* Larchmont, NY: Eye On Education

Rodgers, C. (2002). Defining reflection: Another look at John Dewey and reflective thinking. *The Teachers College Record, 104*(4), 842–866.

Schraw, G., & Moshman, D. (1995). Metacognitive theories. *Educational Psychology Review, 7*(4), 351–371.

Shulman, L. S. (1986). Those who understand: Knowledge growth in teaching. *Educational Researcher, 15*(2), 4–14.

Shulman, L. (1987). Knowledge and teaching: Foundations of the new reform. *Harvard Educational Review, 57*, 1–22.

Senge, P. (1990). *The fifth discipline: The art and science of the learning organization.* New York, NY: Currency Doubleday.

Smith, W. K., & Lewis, M. W. (2001). Toward a theory of paradox: A dynamic equilibrium model of organizing. *Academy of Management Review, 36*(2), 381–403.

Sternberg, R. J. (1985). *Beyond IQ: A triarchic theory of human intelligence.* Cambridge, UK: Cambridge University Press.

Sullivan, P., Smith, M., & Matusov, E. (2009). Bakhtin, Socrates and the carnivalesque in education. *New Ideas in Psychology, 27*(3), 326–342.

Tannen, D., & Leapman, M. (1998). *The argument culture: Changing the way we argue and debate.* London, UK: Virago Press.

Tillema, H., & Kremer-Hayon, L. (2005). Facing dilemmas: Teacher-educators' ways of constructing a pedagogy of teacher education. *Teaching in Higher Education, 10*(2), 203–217.

Vygotsky, L. (2006). *Mind in society: Development of higher psychological processes* (New Ed ed.). Cambridge, MA: Harvard University Press.

Wangaard, D. (n.d.). Moral knowing, moral feeling, moral action. *SEE News. 3*(4). Retrieved from http://ethicsed.org/moral-knowing

Watt, S. K. (2007). Difficult dialogues, privilege and social justice: Uses of the privileged identity exploration (PIE) model in student affairs practice. *College Student Affairs Journal, 26*(2), 114–126.

Windschitl, M. (2002). Framing constructivism in practice as the negotiation of dilemmas: An analysis of the conceptual, pedagogical, cultural, and political challenges facing teachers. *Review of Educational Research, 72*(2), 131–175.

CPSIA information can be obtained
at www.ICGtesting.com
Printed in the USA
BVOW06s0052010917
493594BV00002B/20/P